Jesus authorized Christians to "*Go ye therefore, and teach all nations, baptizing them in the name of the Father, and of the Son, and of the Holy Ghost: Teaching them to observe all things whatsoever I have commanded you: and, lo, I am with you alway, even unto the end of the world. Amen.*"

—Matthew 28:19-20

Matthew 28:19-20

SOULWINNING 101

A Practical Approach
in
Doing the Great Commission

www.GoSoulwinning.com

Matthew 28:19-20

SOULWINNING 101

A Practical Approach

in

Doing the Great Commission

Lawrence W. Bowman

Go Soulwinning Ministries

All scripture quotations are taken from the *King James Version* (KJV) of the Holy Bible.

SOULWINNING 101 A Practical Approach in Doing the Great Commission

ISBN-13: 9780615522128
ISBN-10: 0615522122
Printed in the United States of America
Copyright © 2011 by Go Soulwinning Ministries

For further information,
you may contact the author at:
www.GoSoulwinning.com
or
www.LawrenceBowman.com
Thank you.

Special big thanks to Sixto J. Serrano with
www.316Production.com
for delineating the illustrations inside this book.

Contents

And ye shall seek me [God], *and find me,*
when ye shall search for me with all your heart.
–Jeremiah 29:13

Dedication

Ask of me [God], *and I shall give thee the heathen for thine inheritance,*
And the uttermost parts of the earth for thy possession.
–Psalm 2:8

I dedicate this book and its series to the one-hundred million souls for whom God has burdened me to pray and believe for; and to the believers who are willing to reach them.

Additionally, there certainly are billions of souls who need to be told that they have offended God by breaking His Law and that they are guilty of sin. These souls need to be told that if they should die right at this moment, they would face the judgment of God and be sentenced to the pit of Hell for all eternity. These souls need to be informed that even though they are guilty of sin, God still loves them, and He loves them so much that He gave His only begotten Son, Jesus, to die on a cross and take the punishment for their guilty sins. These souls need to be told that Jesus was buried and then He victoriously resurrected the third day. These souls need to be compelled to believe on Jesus for the forgiveness of their sins and receive God's gift of eternal life.

I pray that each soul that is directly or indirectly touched by this book and its series will become wholly devoted to God.

May you, Christian, rise up to the divine commandments and invest your life into the life of another person by preaching the Gospel and compelling them to look unto the Lord Jesus Christ!

Acknowledgments

Render therefore to all their dues: tribute to whom tribute is due;
custom to whom custom; fear to whom fear; honour to whom honour.
— Romans 13:7

I make no claim to originality for any of the writings or teachings in this book. The truths that I present to you in this book have been passed down for many of hundreds and thousands of years. I have only come along today in present times and modernized what many former men of God, teachers, and even some of my personal mentors have spoken in time past.

In my personal studies, I enjoy reading books and notes of the great preachers, evangelists, and orators of God's Word such as: George Whitefield, Charles Spurgeon, Charles Finney, Dr. Jack Hyles, Dr. John Rice, and many more. I also enjoy studying over observations and notes of my own personal mentors. I acknowledge that my material is not all original. I have gleaned my knowledge from these mighty men of God. I have intertwined discourses and sermon notes from Charles Spurgeon, writings from Dr. Jack Hyles, insight from Charles Finney, lectures from Dr. John R. Rice, passages and paragraphs from numerous other religious and spiritual commentators and their books into this book along with my words.

I am not an original thinker. I am not that smart. I have founded no school of scriptural interpretation or application. I have not given any new exposition of Bible passages, nor have I developed any lines of thought or illustrations. The certainty is that no one will hear anything new from me. I have taken the truths taught to me by my mentors and scholars of old and combined all their teachings regarding Christ's Great Commission in Matthew 28:19-20 and have adapted and paraphrased and modernized them. The qualified reader will be able to detect my tone of voice interwoven with the wisdom and knowledge taught by other respectable men of God.

By the way, I by no means equal myself to any one of my mentors. I only seek to exalt and preach the same simple and powerful Gospel of our Lord Jesus Christ and to equip and edify other Christians through the teachings of His Word. I thank and praise God so much for the men He has positioned around me in my life. God has used these individuals to change my heart for the better; that I may increase in the knowledge of God, that I may walk worthy of the Lord unto all pleasing, and that I may be fruitful in every good work with the lives of people around me.

I express great appreciation and praise to God for His Gospel, for saving me, for His Great Commission, and for allowing us to be entrusted with His Gospel. I express appreciation to all the men who have gone before me and who are working today for His Kingdom. I praise God that I have had the opportunities to learn from these men. May the Lord Jesus be praised and glorified, and even that much more!

I also express my appreciation to a few other people whom God has permitted to be a blessing to me with the preparations of this book. Whether they realize it or not, God certainly has used them in my life. Those individuals are Ruth Wade Wright, Bill Pierce, Tom Cantor, Penny Bowman, David Perry, Joshua Humphrey, and many others.

Thank you so very much,

CHAPTER 1
My Story

Come and hear, all ye that fear God,
and I will declare what he hath done for my soul.
– Psalm 66:16

I want to begin by first thanking you for bringing the topic of soulwinning to your attention through the reading of this book. It is in my heartfelt prayers and my deepest hopes that you will gain much insight in biblical wisdom and doctrinal knowledge in the truths that God desires for you to know and to do concerning His Gospel.

Perhaps you may be thinking in your mind that since I am the individual who put this book together that I must know all there is to understand about the topic of soulwinning. On the contrary, I confess that such an assumption would be erroneous. I must disappoint such an assumption and acknowledge that though God has permitted me to understand some of the immense treasures of soulwinning, I, too, still have much learning, searching and seeking in the holy scriptures to apply His Word with the Holy Spirit's guidance for greater and deeper means of serving with Jesus through soulwinning.

Though I endeavor to have a soulwinning lifestyle in my personal affairs, I still have had to read, study, and meditate on many truths in the provisions such as those found in this book. God has mercifully broadened my understandings and He has mercifully given me practical revelation about His work of guiding souls to Christ through my immense hours of readings, studies, and writings for this book combined with my personal experiences and services with the Lord Jesus Christ. The Holy Bible teaches us in Hebrews 10:24 that we should consider ways to provoke one another on toward love and good deeds. As I have spent hundreds of hours putting together this book, I have felt God's eye of examination, and He has shown me different ways that you and I can provoke one another to love and toward good works in the actions of daily soulwinning.

I write to you in order to excite you to be a God-dependent, effectual soulwinner just as many of my personal mentors and pupils have spurred me to do. I wholeheartedly hope that the knowledge in this book may provoke you into greater joys and experiences in knowing Jesus through the choices and actions of winning souls unto Christ. There have been many instances during the process of putting this book together where I was studying, meditating, or typing, and all of the sudden I have had to stop what I was doing, get down on my knees and speak with the Lord about the topics now found in this book. In my many talks with the Lord, I have had to acknowledge my own personal errors and needs. I have had to supplicate for wisdom and guidance in my own life's actions. There have been many times when I have had to stop typing and acknowledge to the Lord Jesus my own failures and shortcomings. I have had to repent of my faults and wonderfully acknowledge my great need for Him. Hallelujah! It is a marvelous time when the Lord deepens our understanding of just how much more we really do need Him. Thank you, God!

It has become a great joy and a personal honor that the Lord Jesus would permit me to study such a worthy topic. I first started this project with the mindset to spur others, but I am gloriously honored and filled with great joy and humility that the Lord Jesus would embrace this project onto my life to provoke me to know Him in a deeper way (2 Corinthians 4:17) too. I thank God so much for His longsuffering and His enormous desire to draw me closer to Himself through His Word, my sufferings, my studies, His joys, and my personal experiences with Him. Oh….and I sincerely hope that you will choose to make the time to get to know God more wonderfully too. You may or may not be given the capacity to write a book, but you certainly can and should choose to seek God through the study of His Word, through time alone in prayer with Him, and through the meditation of His Word. I hope you surely do those necessities in your life as well. What a rich reward you will be given from God! I say all of that because one very important objective that God has through the work of soulwinning is for us to become more intimate with Him. God desires for us to know Him so much more in a wonderful way and to experience a dynamic love relationship with Him. He wants us to come closer to Him that we might know Him more. Philippians 3:10 informs us that all these provisions are so that WE MAY KNOW HIM. Therefore, I exhort you to seek to know Christ in your preparations and in your actions of soulwinning.

I certainly can testify that God has used soulwinning as one powerful method to alter my thinking and to bring me personally closer to Him. Nevertheless, years before I ever began to invest my life into the life of another individual, and years before I importuned myself to tell someone else about the Lord Jesus Christ, little did I know, God had been working to draw me to Himself. I now realize with certainty that, just as He has taken my lifetime to draw me to Himself, He too has been doing the same in your life as well.

My short life story begins with my mother's pregnancy with me back in the late 1970's. She had a fairly normal and good pregnancy up until her last month. Unlike her ideal pregnancy with my sibling, she developed major complications carrying me, and during her whole last month of pregnancy she was not permitted to walk or so suffer the unwanted dire consequences. Then, during the delivery of me, my mother's complications went from very bad to nearly fatal. She began hemorrhaging profusely. Her vital signs were quickly depreciating. The doctors hurriedly performed a cesarean section and I was pulled out from the warmth and safety of my mother into the cold and complicated world. Praise the LORD that God permitted the doctors to quickly work on my mother and me, as we were both saved. God permitted those sufferings and altercations and through them gave me the wonderful gift of life on this tiny planet that we humans call Earth. I was blessed to be born to the parents Walter and Penny Bowman in Columbus, Ohio. My parents decided to name me after my mother's sagacious father, Lawrence Wesley Drummond; and so I was privileged with the name Lawrence Wesley Bowman. Lawrence Wesley, after my grandfather, and Bowman, after my father.

I can remember that while I was growing up that my mother consistently took my brother John and I to church every Sunday. My father very rarely attended church services until I was ten years old. The church we attended preached Jesus and sound doctrine from the Holy Bible. Although the pastor did include the Gospel message into all of his sermons, I did not become submissively obedient to the Gospel message until I was a teenager. Nonetheless, I am appreciative that we went to church faithfully, because if it were not for that, I probably would not have heard the Gospel hundreds of times, nor would have met those few important individuals who God used to influence me to have concern about my soul and be responsive toward God's Word.

In other areas of my childhood life, I was very blessed to be raised in a family that made efforts to support and encourage me to do well in school. I can remember all the countless instances of me volunteering my mother to help out at school events and student projects and then seeing my mother actually following through what I had signed her up to do without her permission. She surely was faithful and very good in her numerous volunteer responsibilities, even to those occasions which I signed her up to help 24 hours before she was supposed to be at the school. She and I now laugh at the uncounted memories because one would have thought she was a paid staff at our school.

I am also extremely appreciative toward God for giving me a father who strongly exemplified a great work ethic before my eyes. My father always has lived a diligent life in being ethical and faithful in working. I think this is one reason why I am blessed with a strong work ethic too. My continuous exposure and observance of his faithfulness and ethics drilled my heart to be the same. My father has been faithful in serving his employment so that my family and I would have food on the table and electricity in the home.

My family and I, as it seems to me, were just another regular Midwestern family who cherished one another and served to get along with our neighbors and strangers around us. It is sad, but that integrity is diminishing all around us in our country today. With all the good and challenging experiences while growing up in my family, the most cherished memories I am fond of are those of the frequent exciting celebrations for our birthdays, Christmases, Easters, and many other holidays. God certainly was good to allow me to grow up in a unique family with good memories. All these memories have helped to shape me to have a desire to have a positive outlook in life.

Although I was for the most part a happy child growing up, my family and I did experience some instances of tensions and challenges. I will not go into detail about our deep felt affairs, as they do not adequately pertain to this book. However, I will briefly mention that there was a period of family happiness mixed with secrets of family pangs, due to the devious destructive spirit of addiction that crept into my mother's life through the introduction of doctor prescribed medications for her health problems. With addiction in the midst of the family, times of tension would abruptly explode, mostly during the night, and create times of drama. Though my family tried to keep this addiction a secret, sometimes the secret could not be hidden and people would become concerned for our family. I praise God that even in the midst of these challenging, startling times, I always had the feeling of love within our family. I personally think that these very difficult times and circumstances occasionally seemed to try to pull us apart, but in the long run I believe that God has used them to bring us closer together as a family. As I look back at it all now, I can see the hand of God working in those questionable times of my life. God was using those challenging times to break both my parent's stubborn self wills and lure them to become dependent on Him.

My mother was the one who had become an addict to pain pills and my father was the brassy individual who expressed his deep concerns through strong arguments with my mother. After struggling through that for some years, my mother saw the divine light and she ultimately surrendered her addiction and sought successful medical godly assistance. During all of this, my father at last surrendered his life to the Lord Jesus Christ immediately following a Sunday morning Christmas Eve church service. God took our circumstances, concerns, and worries, and carried us through them all. God used all these concerns to draw us closer to Himself so that the Bowman family would come to be under His perfect influence and guidance in our lives.

The day my father received Jesus as His personal Savior brought much rejoicing to my family. It was the greatest Christmas gift that any of us could have received. My mother had prayed for my father for many years that he would call upon Jesus for salvation. And finally, that day arrived! Hallelujah!

I can vividly remember the time when my father gave his life to Jesus Christ. I remember that there was a significant and distinctive immediate change in his demeanor and speech. He even stopped smoking right away. My father began to pick up his Bible every single day and read and talk about it. The atmosphere of our home seemed to transform from mixed happiness to a calm joyous peace. I do not mean it was a perfect heavenly oasis, but just in general there was this better, God-centered atmosphere noticeable within the home. The whole family began attending church services together, and my father would talk to us and watch Bible-centered preaching on the television with us.

After my father surrendered his life to Jesus, he faithfully started to read the Bible every day. I also remember many people at my church telling me that I should read the Bible as well. Many times my pastor and other adults would tell me how great a book the Bible is. Two ladies at my church are most memorable. These ladies would very frequently encourage me to read it so that I could hear God's voice. They would tell me of things that God was saying to them through their times in the Bible and that spurred a desire within me to want to hear God's voice, too. Although I started to grow interest in what all these people were telling me, I had not yet started to apply what I was hearing. I did on occasion pick up the Bible and read parts here and there, but for the most part, I did not pay much attention to their suggestions. I thought the Bible was too difficult and too big to understand and therefore I questioned why I should try to learn what I did not understand. On the contrary, today I now understand that is the very reason why we should read the Bible! How can we learn unless we engage our hearts in hearing truths that we yet do not understand? If only I would have understood this wisdom back then! How I thank God so much for His patience and for sending His persistent messengers to remind me over and over to pick up the Bible and read it!

Then my father gave his life to Jesus and right before my very eyes I witnessed a man who was a high school dropout, who did not know anything about the Bible, begin to read it and actually start to understand and even to engage in good conversations about what he was learning. The Lord used my father's salvation and my father's faithful actions in the daily reading of his Bible to stir more of an interest inside of me. I do not know if my father realized it at the time, but I was carefully watching him like a predator watches its prey. I started to think that perhaps I could be like my father, and read the Bible and understand it too. Finally, one day after seeing him read the Bible consistently, faithfully every day, hearing him talk about it, and then noticing a change in his character,

I gave up my pathetic attitude and sometime during my twelfth year of life I chose to pick up the daily Bible-reading habit! I decided that I would read the Bible every evening before I would go to sleep. I am happy to testify that I did this very thing faithfully.

Each night I would get in my bed and would make the time to read one chapter. I consistently did this every evening, even during the many times I did not understand what I was reading. Even so, I stayed faithful to my reading; praise the Lord! If I did not understand something I was reading, I would continue to read the words and go on faithfully with the reading. Nonetheless, I did discover that most of the stories I read were enjoyable and graphically written in detail. Though I did not understand everything I read, I did realize that I was beginning to learn a little bit more of what was inside of the Bible. There were many times that I did not understand what I was reading, but I thought that even though I did not understand everything, it still would be beneficial to continue reading the Bible.

Over the next several years without my awareness, God was using His Word to mold and shape my heart for a deeper relationship with Him. I was going on with my normal life, and at night reading His Word, and God in the background of my life and in my heart was patiently chiseling away unwholesome thoughts and attitudes of mine, and He was slowly revealing areas of Himself to me that would whet my appetite to want to know more of Him. My good and bad experiences together with my daily Bible reading were the beginning of a major change within my heart. I did not become conscious about even the slightest of what He had already been doing in my heart until I was around fifteen and half years old. Around this age, it seems to me that God started to bring upon my heart conviction. I had never felt or known about His conviction on one's heart, so I ignorantly blew it off and ignored it for a while. Thankfully, God was longsuffering with me and numerous times when I would read the Bible or when I would hear the pastor preaching at church I would feel uncomfortable inside myself. I do not speak about feeling uncomfortable physically, as if I were too cold or too hot. It was if I could feel a type of uncomfortable consciousness within my heart, as if I were in the wrong and needed divine help. I now know that this uncomfortable consciousness is the Lord's guidance of conviction. The best way I can try to explain what I was feeling is perhaps comparing it to the feeling of a tug or pull on my heart during these times. This tug was a conviction and I continued for many months to wrestle with this divine call of change. I desired to understand why I felt this and what I needed to do to bring amends or correction. Interestingly enough, I never discussed these thoughts and concerns of mine with anyone. I did, however, continue to read my Bible and attend church services, though, this was where the tugs seemed to climax. I always remembered that my pastor had mentioned that all of the answers to our questions are inside the Bible and, therefore, I believed that if I would continue to read the Bible and hear the Bible preached at church that my questions would be answered to why I felt this unsettling within my heart.

Hallelujah! The answers started to be revealed to me after a few months of conviction. As I would read the Bible, and many times at church, I would perceive or perhaps even hear God's voice within my heart. The words I would hear often would tell me that I was not a Christian and that I was on my way to Hell. However, I did not know it was God talking to me. For a long time, though God was providing me the answers which I desired to know, I did not recognize that these "thoughts" were the answers, and so I ignored them and tried to think about something else. I rejected such thoughts that I was not a Christian. I rejected considering that I was not on my way to Heaven and if I were to have died in that moment that I would have gone to Hell. Such thinking was ludicrous to me because I believed that as long as I attended church faithfully, read my Bible, and intellectually understood that Jesus was the Savior, all of those things would earn me the right to go to Heaven.

I refused to believe that all my good works did not count me worthy to
be one of God's children, a Christian. I over and over again struggled
to convince myself that I was a Christian; because I had talked myself
into believing that I was indeed a "good" person and my "good" deeds
should help Jesus to permit me go to Heaven when I die.

Oh how wrongfully self-righteous and religious were my beliefs!
Yet, God was very patient with me. He continued to lovingly convict
me and repeat over and over to me through the weeks that I was not
a Christian, that I was on my way to Hell! These weeks turned into
months; and then finally one day while I was reading the Bible I came
across a passage of scripture that made me stop and to really consider
and think about what it meant in my personal life. I read Ephesians 2:8-
9, *"For by grace are ye saved through faith; and that not of yourselves:
it is the gift of God: Not of works, lest any man should boast."* When I
read these two verses, it was as if the words on the page literally jumped
off the paper and slapped me across the face. I had to halt my reading.
Though I did not first understand what they meant to me, I knew that
I had come across something important in the Bible. I knew that there
was something that I had to understand, but I did not know what it was
at first. Therefore, I reread and reread and reread these two verses over
and over again. I pondered about what they meant and the reason why I
wanted to know what they were saying. As I really thought about what
each word meant I came to realize that the words related to my personal
life. It started to make sense to me! This excited me because I felt as if
I was learning something profound from my own reading of the Bible
instead of some man telling me what it meant. It was exciting to see
that God's own Word, the Holy Bible, was trying to tell me something
important. The point it was trying to tell me was that I had a seriously
big problem.

As I considered that I had a problem and as I repetitively reread
the two verses, I realized my problem—I was a sinner. It became clear

to me that an individual does not nor cannot base his Christianity on church attendance nor on any "good" deeds. It became clear to me that a Christian is someone who comes to God through faith, but not faith in his own self. Nor is it a faith in someone else or something else, but faith only in the work and Person of the Lord Jesus Christ. This means that an individual wholeheartedly believes on the Lord Jesus and trusts in His sacrificial work on the cross and His victorious resurrection—to have access to God. Yes, I had believed that Jesus died on the cross and rose from the grave, but all my beliefs were intellectually in my brain. They were not of my heart. It started to become real to me that faith is belief within the heart, not the mind. I started to realize that I had to believe with my heart, because the heart is where passion and convictions of belief are held within an individual, not the mind. Just as I truly believe with conviction and passion that Penny Bowman is my mother, I must have this same type of passion and belief that Jesus really is my need and my Savior.

As I continued to consider these two verses and to contemplate on their meaning in my life I soon understood that salvation with God is free. Salvation has no strings attached and is given to any person, not because the person warrants or deserves it, but because God wants to give the gift of salvation; eternal life to whosoever shall receive it.

As I read the two verses over and over, I realized that me going to church, me reading my Bible, or me trying to do good, was not how I nor anyone else could ever attain the free gift of eternal life from God. For all these so called "good actions" are indeed "works" that people can and definitely should do in life to demonstrate their appreciation, but all these good works certainly cannot attain nor help us at all in becoming a Christian. They do not assist in the slightest bit in earning God's favor. And why is that? Because I, like everyone else in this world, have fallen short of God's perfect standard and we all have disobeyed His fundamental Law, The Ten Commandments. Therefore, we are sinners guilty of breaking God's Law. As I continued to think about this problem, I understood that I indeed had broken God's Law. For example, God commanded us that we are not to lie, nor are we to steal, and that we are to honor our father and our mother (Exodus 20). These are just three of God's Commandments, and yet, these three I knew I had disobeyed and therefore I was guilty for not doing what He commanded me to do. Oh, how sorrowful my heart felt as I realized that I was a sinner and in need of the Savior Jesus Christ! Oh, my heart felt deep trouble and fear of the punishment of Hell. My thoughts began to be filled with fear because I did not want to go to Hell. I did not want to be separated from God for all eternity because I had disobeyed Him. I did not want to burn in the fire forever and rightly experience the punishment for my sins that I chose to do.

I remember asking God the question, "How then can I become a Christian and not go to Hell?" I remember keeping these questions and thoughts to myself and earnestly seeking God to show me the answer. It was not until over a week later when the answer to my questions was revealed to me. Throughout the week and a half I was in deep contemplation and I continued to faithfully read my Bible with the hopes that perhaps I might find the answer to my question, just as I had learned that I was on my way to Hell.

God certainly heard my questions. He certainly brought the answer to my questions just at the right time. I do not remember what time of the day it was, but on one occasion, I was reading the book of Romans in the Holy Bible and I soon came upon the answer to my questions, Romans 10:9-10. The verses state, "*That if thou shalt confess with thy mouth the Lord Jesus, and shalt believe in thine heart that God hath raised him from the dead, thou shalt be saved. For with the heart man believeth unto righteousness; and with the mouth confession is made unto salvation* [forgiveness of sin]." When I came across these verses in my reading I knew I had come across something of great importance because, just as my experience with Ephesians 2:8-9, these verses seemed to jump off the page too. I reread these verses for a better clarity and understanding of them. It promptly became clear to me that this passage of scripture went right along with what Ephesians 2:8-9 explains. As I reread Romans 10:9-10 I came to realize that I had to first believe in Jesus, that He is God the Son and that God the Father raised Him from the dead after Jesus' death and burial. Just as I thought about a little the week before, I understood that I had to believe this with all my heart and not just my mind. And I did believe that. I was convinced of this truth within my heart. Then as a result of my belief, it should and would just make sense to do what the Bible says: I had to personally confess (or acknowledge) my sins before God. I had to repent of my sins and want to follow Jesus. I thought about what all of this meant for the whole day.

As a result of this understanding, in the evening riding home in the car with my parents I made mention to them that I had been thinking a lot about salvation and that I felt I needed to be saved. Actually, my words were to my parents in the car as we were arriving home in the driveway, "I want to be saved." My parents sincerely but sincerely incorrectly believed that I was saved and they erroneously told me, "Son, you are already saved. You went up to the altar when you were four years old." I responded back to them, "Yeah, everybody tells me that, but I don't remember doing that. I don't feel saved. God told me that I need to be saved." My father answered back with misunderstanding, "If you say so. Then you know what to do son." We continued this conversation as we walked into our home. My mother had to get upstairs, so she went ahead of us up the stairs, but I urged my father to pray with me. He hesitated but decided he would pray with me. He and I walked through the living room and into our dining room. We got on our knees in front of one of the dining room chairs and out loud I told God, "Jesus, I am sorry for all of my sins that I have done. I admit that I am guilty and that I have sinned against You. Please forgive me. I really believe with my heart that You died on a cross for me. I do believe that You physically arose from the dead for me. Would You be my Savior and come live in my heart today?" My prayer was that short and simple, yet I wholeheartedly believed with my heart and meant every word that I spoke to Him. No longer did I just believe in Jesus with my mind, but I transferred that belief into my heart. God heard me and came to live inside of me that day. HALLELUJAH! Another great thing that happened at that moment—my fear of dying and going to Hell somehow disappeared. I had this peace of knowing that if I were to die that I would not go to Hell but I would be with my Lord Jesus in Heaven.

Since that day when I placed all my trust in Jesus Christ for salvation, I have continued to have the same indescribable peace that comes from God alone. God has increasingly become more real to me. Praise God that He did not just save me from Hell and stop there and leave me alone. No, God has continued to work within my heart and in my life to edify me in more of Himself and to experience Him in mightier ways which have built up my faith in believing with stronger confidence in the written promises He can accomplish in and through my life.

Sometime after my salvation, I remember reading in my Bible a passage of scripture from the book of Jeremiah. The verses were Jeremiah 29:11-13. They really stuck with me. I was in awe to learn from them that God is presently thinking about me. Not only was I in awe of that, but I also learned His thoughts of me are plans of peace and not evil, to give me a future and a hope. In those verses, I discovered my first promises that I could claim back to God because He promised them. I learned that if I would seek Him with my whole heart and not play games with Him, then He would allow me to find deeper intimacies and treasures of Him. I had already found Him as my Savior, but as I thought about these verses I realized that He really would allow me to come closer to Him and enjoy Him in more meaningful ways; that I could understand more about Him and not just be in bewilderment about

God. This truth overwhelmed me with joy and it built a stronger desire for me to know Him. I wanted to know Him more so that I could find what He wanted in my life. Then, He could accomplish His thoughts of peace and a future in my life. I walked away from this passage grasping a new life objective: that I should and would seek God more and try to get to know Him for the all the days of my life.

As a result of that day and forward I praise God that He has helped me to continue on that goal in seeking Him daily in my life. Although I have not been perfect, He has drawn me closer to Himself everyday through being in His Word daily and through my life's experiences. I admit that I have made many, and perhaps I should emphasize the word, MANY, mistakes. Sometimes, I shamefully admit that I have ignored what I knew in my heart God was telling me to do. Nonetheless, He has been so gracious and so very longsuffering with me. His guidance and His loving corrections have instructed me on forward to a closer walk with Him.

Throughout the years I have known Jesus as my Savior; I have continued to read my Bible on a daily basis. I used to read it at nighttime before I went to bed. Sometime a few years after my conversion, I noticed a pattern amongst holy men and women in the passages of the Holy Bible. They would meet God in the morning before their days began. I do not remember when I made the change, but I decided that it probably would be wise for me to meet God in the mornings as well. As a result, since then, the very first thing I do in my mornings is to spend time alone with God in prayer and reading His Word. I am glad that I have put into practice this habit. Many times God has given me an important word for myself or for someone else that I would meet in that particular day for which there was a need of that particular encouragement. God always knows the future. He knows what the day is going to bring forth before we know.

As I continued to read my Bible, I eventually started desiring to know more of His Word, which reading alone cannot provide. God brought a man into my life who taught me how I can expand my knowledge of God's Word through simple study methods of His Word. Most of the times my favorite type of study has been the method of studying a particular word in the Bible, known as a "Word Study." I have always had many questions. The more studies I do the more of my questions have been answered; which interestingly enough have turned into more questions and more studies. This has been very beneficial in my life. Studying the Bible has enlarged my awe of God and given me a greater appreciation for who He is and what He can and will do.

Not only has the Lord allowed me to study His Word, but also He put a desire for me to witness to people. One such time when I was trying to witness to some people, I did not do a good job. I tried to show the individuals from the Bible what I was saying but I could not find the verse that I knew was indeed in the Bible. The persons walked away from me thinking I did not know what I was talking about and they did not get saved. Frankly, I walked away from our conversation realizing that I was indeed ignorant of God's Word and that maybe I should pick up the habit of memorizing scriptures like a friend of mine had told me to do in my earlier college days. Consequently, I began slowly to memorize verses from the Bible. I say slowly because at first I was not good at it. It seemed so difficult to make a verse stick in my brain. God had seen my zeal, but He understood something I did not know. God realized that I was lacking an important principle concerning His Word: meditation.

God soon brought another man into my life who reminded me of a biblical principle that I had once heard about in Bible teachings. He reminded me that all my Bible readings, studies, and memorizations are important, but the thing I need most of all is to meditate on God's Word. He taught me how to just think, ponder, and examine on a Bible passage or verse. Not just for a few minutes, but to take my time and just meditate about it for a whole day, week, or some extended period of time—time sufficient to assist me to get the true meaning and application of a verse for my life. And no, I do not mean the worldly viewpoint of meditation by laying on the ground, in some sort of stance, with my eyes shut in complete silence. On the contrary, the godly (correct) way to meditate means to go through our normal routines of life and all the while think about and ponder on some certain scripture. God's way of meditation is productive. The world's way is unproductive.

Since I learned that, as I go throughout my normal days now, I consider what a verse means to me, how it applies, what is God trying to say to me, and what I need to do in response to the verse. When I started to meditate on verses that I was trying to memorize, I quickly discovered that my problem was not that I could not memorize; my problem was that I lacked understanding of the verses. My memorization skills grew and God started to give me some wisdom. Meditating on God's Word day and night is where I personally have discovered the deepest treasures of God's promises and revelation. Meditating on God's Word has assisted me in more ways than I could ever imagine. It has helped me get through difficult days. It has allowed me to better serve and minister to people that I meet throughout my days. It has given me that deeper joy of the Lord that only comes by deeply pondering on His Word. It now seems that Isaiah 50:4 has come true in my life: *"The Lord GOD hath given me the tongue of the learned, that I should know how to speak a word in season to him that is weary: he wakeneth morning by morning, he wakeneth mine ear to hear as the learned."* I can thank God for this all because of Bible meditation.

Throughout the years, I have continued to faithfully attend a local church and get involved in the lives of other people. As I pursued spending extra time with God in His Word and fellowshipping with other Christians, it became obvious to me that another essential way of getting to know Jesus better is by involving my life into the lives of others around me. I understood that this meant to invest my time and resources into other lives. God really made it clear through a lot of passages of scripture that this is essential for a Christian to keep growing in Him. Certainly there are many verses which speak on this subject, but two verses that really stand out the most to me are 2 Timothy 2:2 and Isaiah 43:4. These verses speak on involving our lives into the lives of others. And when we do that, God promises an awesome promise—a residual collection of PEOPLE!

As I thought about these verses more and more I recalled the people which God had placed into my life to guide me closer to Himself and His Word. Then I recalled their examples. Certainly, I have memories of a few godly men who have truly lived the Bible in front of me. One man in particular, David Perry, I can say invested much of his life into mine. These verses have filled me with gratitude that God brought David and his wife Sandy into my life. David and Sandy lived the Bible before of me. For example, on a countless number of occasions David has spent much time with me in God's Word either in person or on the phone teaching me things I need to know. David and Sandy both have helped me with many of life's mundane problems. David has trained God's Word into my life through interactions with other people, not just isolation with him. Both of them have opened up their home to me, and so much more. All of these experiences along with the examples of godly men's stories in the Bible compelled my heart that I too need to take my energy, my time and my possessions and use them as an investment to help at least another man come to know Jesus in a dynamic way too. I did not know how to do this, and quite frankly I still do not think I know what I am doing, but I have been learning more and more to just give of myself, time and possessions to men who have a desire to know Jesus. Matthew 20:28 encourages me very much in serving people. It says that Jesus, the King of kings, did not come to be served but to serve men, even to the point of death. I am compelled to serve others because if the King of kings came to serve us humans, than how much more do I need to serve and invest my life into the lives of others? For this reason I am full of gratitude and compelled to give my life and my resources so that others may know Christ and know Him more (Colossians 1:28).

Over time God has been allowing me to not just teach principles from His Word, but to live them in front of people and to train a few men to go out and do the same. God has been allowing me to invest my time and efforts in the training of men so that they can know Him in a dynamic way and then go out and invest their lives into the life of another, too. For example, I felt the conviction in my heart a while back to actively go out and tell others the Gospel of Jesus at people's front doorsteps. So, I started doing this type of evangelism. Meanwhile God has been permitting me to use this time of evangelism to train other men in how to effectually express their faith to others. It has been a really good and powerful blessing. I have found it to not only be an effective way of getting the Gospel to nonbelievers, but also a useful time to disciple and mentor other men.

This book and its series were birthed through this type of personal evangelism and discipleship. One evening as I was working with a guy, he kept asking me many good questions regarding how he could be a more useful instrument in God's hands. I was enjoying his questions. His questions were encouraging to me as I was listening and answering them because I knew that the type of questions he was asking meant that he was catching on to some important truths in the Bible. I could tell that he was hungry for more precious truth, which is always a good thing. And so, I wanted to recommend a book to him to read along with his Bible, but at that time I could not think of any. Though I knew of some good books that could guide him a little, I could not think of any one particular book, that in my opinion, which had been written with answers concerning some of his questions. I could not think of any titles that really demonstrated through words how someone could come to soulwin in a practical and effective manner in regards to what he was asking.

I did what any wise man should do, I recommended him to be a student of the Word and study certain sections of the Bible that pertained to his questions. Nonetheless, the void in my mind of a good book to recommend to him stayed on my mind. Over the next few days of praying and thinking about this dilemma, an outrageous thought ran across my mind. I had a thought that maybe I should take on the task of putting together a book about soulwinning based on the points in the Great Commission of Matthew 28:19-20. Except, that seemed ludicrous to me. There were already so many books out there about soulwinning and the Great Commission, why in the world would God inspire another one? So, I dismissed the idea. I went about my prayers and normal things of life. But over time, the consideration of me writing a book would not leave the back of my thoughts. Therefore, I began to pray about this far-fetched idea, and what would you know, I felt a sense that perhaps I should try to put something together. I got the sense of seriousness and that what I was thinking should become a reality. However, I had some concerns. My concerns were that if I would put together a book, I would want it to include some practical answers about what soulwinning is, who is to do it, why do it, where to do it, when to do it, and most importantly how to do it proficiently and effectively. I would want the book to be so practical that even a fourth grader could read it and use the knowledge and wisdom to win souls for Christ. As I thought about this, my interests grew more and more and so I began to do some research. Through my studies I reexamined my own life and thought about all the important points and principles that God had imparted into me through other's teachings, trainings, and studies. I asked God what He wanted— if He would have me to put a book together about soulwinning. I sensed that if I were to put together a book it should possess theology blended with much biblical doctrine and a whole lot of practical and applicable explanation, information, and examples so that whoever should read the material would be able to practically apply the truths into their daily lives. Since those early thoughts and conversations with the Lord, my prayers have been that people would receive the knowledge, that they would incorporate it and apply the truths into their lives.

I designed an outline for the basis of a single book. I then began to put words down onto paper, and over time, I slowly worked on the project. During the process something extraordinary happened, which is another awesome story in itself. In short, God divinely altered my work on one single book and formed it into the work of four books.

I must say that it has taken me much patience, diligence, a little longsuffering, great sorrows, much prayer, and much study of God's Word to see this work come to pass. All the way through I have been amazed at seeing God's hand bringing it together. I only allowed very few individuals to know that I was writing. Those people were faithful not to talk about this project with anyone else. God was gracious numerous times to encourage me to continue on the project through different ways when sometimes I felt that I should put it away. But many times, and I do not think the people have realized it, God was instrumental in bringing people into my life who had a divine word of encouragement for me or the essential information that I needed at that particular time. For example, one brother in the Lord one day came up to me and handed me about thirty sheets of paper with some good biblical information on them. He, at the time, was not aware that I was writing a book. He, at the time, did not know that I was in prayer that day over a particular topic in my book. And, this is what his words were to me when he approached me and gave me the sheets of paper, "Brother Lawrence, I've been studying on 'such and such topic' and I printed this off for you. I thought you might be interested in reading this too." I looked at the papers, and the topic of the printed material was nothing that seemed to interest me at the time, but I told him that I would look at them sometime at home. The next day I picked up his printed material and began to read it. Though the subject of the material did not interest me, yet it contained some valuable biblical references and statements that went right along with what I had been praying about the day before. Some of the information helped me with one of the chapters.

Many other instances of this sort have occurred. I could mention to you example after example of the many times that God has provided me with knowledge and understanding concerning the topic of this book. But I will not. It is sufficient to say that God has done them in just the most unique wonderful ways that it is totally impossible to not think that God divinely stepped in and brought the right people and the right materials to me at each right time. This is the reason why I cannot and will not foolishly claim that I put this book or its series together. I believe without a shadow of doubt that this book is the Lord's doing. God inspired me to write it. God brought the helps to bring all of it together. God gave me the patience, the persistence, the brains, and the heart to put it together. I thank Him very much for choosing and permitting me to be an instrument to help bring attention to the topic of soulwinning to Christians around the world. Jesus Christ deserves all praise and thanks for this work and many other works that will come about because of this work.

As you already know, I am human. I admit it. Consequently, I am sure there is something that I have left out. Or, perhaps there might be a point that could be explained better. Though this be true, I hope you learn much practical truths from this book and its series. I have not written these books to be a mere theology of soulwinning. More importantly, I sincerely hope and deeply pray that you will apply these methods, tools, points, principles, examples, and exhortations from the Bible into your own personal life. I also hope and pray that you will GO APPLY into your life what you learn! If you do not apply what you learn then you will quickly forget what you learned and you will have wasted your time and God's resources. Please do not be guilty of wasting your time and efforts. However, if you do apply these truths to your life, I know that God will honor your obedience and faithfulness. He will allow you to reap in the souls of His harvest—for the fields are ripe for harvest (Matthew 9:37). The laborers are few. Therefore, rise up and become a laborer for the Lord's harvest. In considering this, there is a verse in the Bible that we ought to consider as we go out and apply these truths into our lives. Psalm 126:5-6 reveals to us, *"They that sow in tears shall reap in joy. He that goeth forth and weepeth, bearing precious seed, shall doubtless come again with rejoicing, <u>bringing his sheaves with him</u>."* People are the sheaves mentioned in this verse. So, go out and bring in the souls of mankind to Jesus. There is much joy, yet at the same time, there is much grief in working in the lives of people to bring them to Jesus. Nonetheless, I have discovered that the joy of the Lord always recompenses for the grief and sorrow of soul bearing.

This book is intended by no means to be a replacement nor a substitute for personal training. This book is written to be merely a teaching guide in the work of the Great Commission. <u>By no means should a man trade training (being involved in another's life) with teaching (reading this book)</u>! In addition, this book is not meant to be a bunch of rules to live by. Instead, it is my hope that this book will inspire you to seek Jesus first (Matthew 6:33), listen to hear His voice (Psalm 46:10), and become sensitive to the Holy Spirit's guidance (Galatians 5:16), and obey Him in what He tells you to do (Jeremiah 7:23). I have put this book together for the intention that Christians may have an editorial to glean and learn from. It is my utmost prayer that new converts will read this book and be compelled to diligently find a godly man or a godly woman to train them in how to implement these biblical truths and methods into their own lives. It is also my prayer that older Christians will use this book as a tool to glean from and be exhorted to find someone to disciple and train. Keep in mind a wise saying that I have heard from one of my mentors and Preacher Steven B. Curington who both have often said, "Most books are written for our information, but the Bible was written for our transformation." How true that is! Please understand that you can read this book, but <u>never substitute man's words over God's words, the Holy Bible</u>. Please, <u>do</u> take the words of this book and compare them to the words of the Holy Bible. Compare the words of this book to the life of Jesus. Also, with utmost attention, do what the Bible says: Matthew 28:19-20 commissions us to GO! Jesus said, *"<u>Go</u> ye therefore, and <u>teach</u> all nations, <u>baptizing</u> them in the name of the Father, and of the Son, and of the Holy Ghost: <u>Teaching</u> them <u>to observe all things whatsoever I have commanded</u> you: and, lo, I am with you alway, even unto the end of the world. Amen."*

PART ONE

THE GOING

CHAPTER 2

What Is Soulwinning?

Whom [Christ] *we preach, warning every man, and teaching every man in all wisdom; that we may present every man perfect in Christ Jesus.*
– Colossians 1:28

I welcome you to the reading of this valuable topic of soulwinning. I do not know where you are, what you do, or who you are, but I do know that God knows you intimately well. Perhaps you are new in your relationship with Jesus Christ and you realize that Christ desires you to serve with Him. Or, perhaps you are on the other extreme. You might be an elder who has known the Lord for quite a long time and you still seek more wisdom and counsel in the King's instructions. Or, maybe you are in the middle somewhere and you are among the numerous Christians who wonder why God never uses them to win a soul to Christ.

Whichever category you fall into, I am thrilled that you are reading this book. Not because I am the author and I think I have something to say, on the contrary. Proverbs 18:2 reveals that my words mean nothing whatsoever. My words are just commentary. But God's Word, the Holy Bible, is truth, therefore, we should study and communicate His truths. And the truths we discover, we are to live out.

If you know Jesus Christ as your Savior, then God authorizes you, as well as myself, to accomplish an important and valuable commission through our lives—That commission is the ministry of reconciliation— soulwinning. Second Corinthians 5:18 says, "[A]*ll things are of God, who hath reconciled us to himself by Jesus Christ, and hath given to us* [Christians] *the ministry of reconciliation.*" You and I have the wonderful responsibility to take the hands of God and man and join them together in Jesus name. This is what soulwinning is all about. Therefore, our main interest in life should be to soulwin. Like a schoolteacher, we need to know a great many things; but just as the schoolteacher must know about children, and how to proficiently educate them, so we must know about souls, and how to win and guide them to Christ. The objective of soulwinning is for God-fearing men and women to go out and tell others about God and the message He has for them and guide them to Jesus in a proficient and effective manner.

And you know what? Soulwinning is one of the most important themes spoken about through the timeless words of the Holy Bible. God clearly teaches about this fundamental topic, its implications, and its practical applications to us through His holy Word. It is a central theme found in every single book of the Bible. For example, in the very beginning of the Bible, in the first book, Genesis, we see God calling upon men to walk near Him and have a relationship with Him. He then orders these same men to proclaim His Word; some such men were Enoch, Noah, and Abram (Abraham). In the following book of the Bible, Exodus, we see God doing the same thing with Moses. As we continue through the Old Testament we see more examples of God carrying out the same theme in His relationship with men such as Joshua in the books of Exodus and Numbers, and Samuel in the book of First Samuel. More examples are found with Zechariah, Ezra, Nehemiah, Isaiah, Jeremiah, Hosea, and Jonah among others. God follows the same theme in the New Testament. We see men such as Stephen, Paul, Philip, Peter, James, and John having a relationship with the Lord, and meanwhile representing Him and proclaiming His Word to the people around them.

Soulwinning is so essential that Jesus majored on it throughout His whole public ministry. Making disciples was the pursuit that weighed so heavily on the heart of Jesus. We see countless stories in the Bible where Jesus trained and ordered His disciples to go out and proclaim His Word. Then Jesus emphasized it during his last talks with His disciples.

One of the major final points Jesus gave special attention to before His departure from this earth back to Heaven dealt with the topic of soulwinning. In His last words, Jesus commissioned His disciples, and subsequently all Christians, through the simple words found in Matthew 28:19-20, to soulwin. He said, *"Go ye therefore, and teach all nations* (The Gospel of Mark's version says, *"[P]reach the gospel to every creature."*), *baptizing them in the name of the Father, and of the Son, and of the Holy Ghost: Teaching them to observe all things whatsoever I have commanded you: and, lo, I am with you alway, even unto the end of the world. Amen."* It is chiefly important that everything a Christian does should first be filtered through this Great Commission. This is to ensure that a Christian's speech, actions, choices, and decisions are correctly aligned into God's priorities. God does have priorities. Though we sometimes fail at aligning ourselves into His priorities, He is faithful and He, with great longsuffering, will remind us of the essentials, if we only listen.

This commission—notably known as the Great Commission within Christendom—from Jesus to all Christians, gets straight to the points of what we are to do as believers. Notice Jesus did not say, "Go ye therefore and make church buildings;" or, "go ye therefore and develop bus ministries;" or, "Go ye therefore and get converts." Yes, all of those activities are wonderful, in proper context. But they should not be the focus of our lives. Instead, notice the words that Jesus instructed us: *"Go ye therefore, and teach all nations, baptizing them in the name of the Father, and of the Son, and of the Holy Ghost: Teaching them to observe all things whatsoever I have commanded you: and, lo, I am with you alway, even unto the end of the world. Amen."* Jesus uses simple language in directing us of what we are to accomplish in our relationship with Him. A relationship with Jesus will always result in the work of soulwinning. In addition, soulwinning is not a program or a curriculum. Jesus commissioned us to do actions which involve us going out and investing our lives into the lives of others instead of sitting around doing nothing. We are to occupy our lives for His Kingdom.

We know this because He used several action verbs in this Great Commission. The first action verb He used in directing us to accomplish His mission is the command, "*Go*." Jesus tells us that we are to go. That means that we are to go where the nonbelievers are. It does not mean to hang up a sign in front of our church, home, or office that reads, "If anybody wants to know Jesus, inquire within." It does not mean to place a bumper sticker on our cars and self-justify that we are doing our duty for the Gospel's sake. Neither does it mean to create flyers or brochures and mail them to a mass audience hoping that they will take the initiative to come to us and find God. No, and, on the contrary, the word "go" means that you are to move or proceed toward the nonbelievers, to go where they dwell, and to create opportunities to be around them. Whether through looking them up and tracking them down or simply walking out of our comfort zones and reaching out to them within our communities in different ways, we are to go. This can and should be done because Jesus said in John 17:18 that He has sent us into the world and since we are left in this world, you and I are to go where they are and witness to them. This means that we are to go when it is comfortable and convenient. But guess what? It also means that we are to go even most assuredly when it is uncomfortable and inconvenient.

You are to go because the whole purpose of the Gospel is to get you involved in another's life (as Jesus did), so that they can have companionship with God and they can also get involved in the life of another. You cannot get involved in other people's lives simply by sitting at home and praying that God will drop some magical, miraculous package of revelation into other people's lives. No, God typically does not do that. Instead, God works in the big majority of people's lives by using people. He has chosen to use people in people's lives to accomplish His will. This is why God calls you and me to go. God always utilizes people in the lives of other people to bring His message and will into their lives.

The second action verb that Jesus used in His Great Commission is, *"Teach"* (and the book of Mark uses the order, *"Preach"*). The term, "teach," means to impart knowledge. The term, "preach," does not mean to scream, it means to proclaim and make known knowledge, especially knowledge of the Gospel. These words are synonyms. We are to teach and preach at the same time, meaning we are to impart and proclaim the knowledge of the Gospel to the world. If you teach or preach, you can win them! However, this involvement is only the preliminary work of soulwinning in the lives of others. It is the initiative to be involved in the course of someone's life. Therefore, we are to take upon ourselves this preliminary responsibility and go out and tell them they are sinners and how they can be saved from the penalty of their sins.

To reiterate, the first thing Jesus commissioned us to do is—*Go*. Then the second thing He commissioned us to do is—*Teach* them the Gospel and compel them to be saved.

The next action verb Jesus used is, *"Baptize."* After we compel them to be saved, we are ordered to baptize our new converts. We are not instructed to sprinkle water on them but to completely baptize them. It is that simple.

And finally Jesus left us the last order with His words: *"...Teaching them to observe all things whatsoever I have commanded you."*

Notice again there are four basic action verbs in Jesus' commission: (1) *Go*; (2) *Teach* (or preach, compelling them to be saved); (3) *Baptize*; and (4) *Teach* them again. These are four divine authorized orders, and they are all simple to obey and do.

This fourth and final command tells us to continue our involvement in people's lives and to impart His truth through our lives by investing our time, energy, possessions, resources, and knowledge into the lives of our new converts. If this last command of the Great Commission is not executed, then the whole work of soulwinning has not been accomplished. For you do not win the soul of an individual until you win his whole body. After someone calls upon the name of Jesus for salvation, we are commissioned to baptize them and to immediately begin teaching and training our new converts wonderful life-altering truths. The points we are to teach them are what Jesus said in His Great Commission, to "...*observe all things whatsoever I have commanded you.*" He did not say to teach "whatsoever I have suggested to you." But He said to teach them "*whatsoever I have commanded you.*" It is not complicated at all. The truths that Jesus commanded us to teach are the three preceding points that He just commissioned. The details Jesus commissioned us to teach are (1) *Go*; (2) *Teach* (proclaim, preach the Gospel); (3) *Baptize*; and (4) *Teach* them what He commissioned us to do. Accordingly, we are to teach our new converts to go, and preach, and baptize, that they may teach their new converts to go, preach and baptize, that they may teach their new converts to go and preach and baptize, and so on. That simple!

In 2 Corinthians 11:3 God informs us that the Gospel is simple. Anyone can go and speak it. In 1 John 5:3 God informs us that His commandments are not grievous, or in other words, burdensome. He made it simple. However, we sadly tend not to believe His work is simple and we try to make it difficult. But, God ordained and designed His Great Commission to be so simple and not grievous that a little child can do it as well. We have such a great commission that we definitely can accomplish it. We just have to act upon what we hear.

Why should we act upon what we hear and do His work? Because, if we fail to do so then it is sin—James 4:17. A Christian who does not act upon what God has commanded is violating God, and in all actuality he is also violating God's purpose (2 Timothy 1:9), God's plan (John 3:16), and God's pleasure (Ezekiel 33:11). Jesus, in Matthew 12:30, warned that a Christian who does not soulwin is demonstrating actions against Him. To live a life that is against God, His pleasure, His plan and His purpose is to live a life that assaults God, and this is treason. God rhetorically asks the right question in Isaiah 14:27: *"For the LORD of hosts hath purposed, and who shall disannul it?"* As if to ask, "Which one of you dares to live a life contrary to My purpose?" We know His purpose because 2 Peter 3:9 tells us that *"[the Lord is] longsuffering to us-ward, not willing that any should perish, but that all should come to repentance."* Thankfully, God is longsuffering toward us. Nonetheless, the truth of the question is that many of us stubbornly fail to soulwin. We live our life and daily assault God and commit treason against Him and His kingdom when we refuse to soulwin. We ought to get down on our knees, repent of our wickedness and thank God for being abundantly longsuffering with us while working with us to accomplish His purpose, His plan, and His pleasure.

Because soulwinning is not a theory, we therefore can live a life that honors God by bringing Him pleasure by fulfilling His purpose through His plan. Such is possible because soulwinning is a mindset, soulwinning is a habit, and soulwinning is a lifestyle. It is these proofs in how a Christian demonstrates his love for God. The Christian demonstrates his love through his obedience to Christ's commission: To actively go out into the world and tell others about Jesus Christ and His Gospel. God warns us three times in the scripture texts of Isaiah 29:13, Matthew 15:8, and Mark 7:6 that we are not to be individuals who merely draw near to Him with our mouths nor to merely honor Him with our lips. The Bible warns that these types of individuals have hearts that are far from Him. God wants more than lip service. God wants our hearts to draw near to Him. He lets us know in 1 Samuel 16:7 that He is a God who pays attention to our hearts rather than the temporal appearance before men. God looks at the heart.

To draw near to God is achieved through our choices and actions rather than our quick responses of words. Later, Jesus taught us how we can draw near and honor God with our hearts. Jesus said in John 14:15: *"If ye love me, keep my commandments."* Our actions prove where our heart is because our actions are stimulated by thoughts and our thoughts are stimulated by the desires of our heart, according to Proverbs 4:23, Matthew 15:18-19, and James 1:14-15. If we are to demonstrate our love toward Jesus by obedience to His commandments, then what were the commandments that He instructed? I am glad you asked. That's an excellent question! The commandments that Jesus set forth can be found in Matthew 22:37-40, which directs us to first love God and secondly to love our neighbors. Later, in Matthew 28:19, He informed us of what we are to do in order to demonstrate obedience to His commands: (1) Go; and (2) Teach all nations the Gospel. If we love God and love our neighbors then we will perform these actions of going and telling the Gospel to people. Yet another time, in Mark 16:15, it is recorded that Jesus commanded us to go unto all the world and preach the Gospel to every creature. So you see, to love God is to demonstrate it through soulwinning.

The point of the matter, and to be frank about it, is that a Christian who does not go and tell others the Gospel is being disobedient to Christ's command. This type of Christian is not proving his love for Jesus. Therefore, it would be a wise idea for us to examine ourselves in order to see if we really love Jesus or not. We should take heed to Jesus' admonishment in Matthew 15:8 and really consider if we are simply giving Him lip service or if we are truly honoring and demonstrating our love towards Him. Are we trying to only honor God with our lips and mouth? Or, are we loving God through actions that are demonstrating obedience by going out and telling the Gospel to others?

Soulwinning is not a formula or a step-by-step event. Neither is soulwinning going out and conveying a plan to people. Soulwinning is telling lost people about the Person Jesus Christ and why we need Him and how we can allow Him into our lives. The initial part of introducing people to the Gospel of Jesus Christ can seem to involve a type of methodology. Nonetheless, we must keep in mind that we are not introducing a method to people; we are simply guiding them to understand their need for the Savior and what they need to do with Him. For example, the Gospel does cover a spectrum of important points. But soulwinners do not go out to introduce a religious plan to the lost. Soulwinners go out to initially tell someone the Gospel. The initial great work of soulwinning is first telling the bad news to others that they have offended God through the breaking of His Law and that their sin merits them worthy of Hell. Then once we cover those points, we are then to tell the good news that people can call upon Jesus for the forgiveness of their guilty sins. Once an individual believes upon Jesus for salvation, soulwinning enters the spectrum of training and teaching the new convert principles in obedience to God. To sum it up, soulwinning is fundamentally telling the news that God has chosen to use a nobody to tell everybody about Somebody (our Lord Jesus) who can save anybody.

The modern-day lifestyle evangelism, also known as friendship evangelism, of only befriending people and hoping that one day in life the opportunity will arise for the lost sinner to ask about their need of salvation is a misnomer. It is a wolf in sheep's clothing idea concocted by the devil and cunningly whispered into the ears of ignorant Christians. The preliminary area of soulwinning, by definition, demands us to open our mouths and preach: purposefully opening your mouth and telling the Gospel to someone. While lifestyle can either hinder or enhance the message we should be telling, it clearly does not preach it for us. Jesus did not say, "Go ye into all the world and live the Gospel before every creature." No. He said, "*Go ye into all the world, and preach* [purposefully tell] *the gospel to* [before] *every creature.*"

Through our living we are to be soulwinning. Whether we are proclaiming, sermonizing, preaching, ministering, serving, proselytizing, evangelizing, outreaching, helping, or witnessing, we are to soulwin. Although, all these terms have semantic differences in reference to the methods of winning the lost for Jesus and guiding people closer to Him, it can be agreed that all these words absolutely have the same great concept of soulwinning. We are not to be a defense attorney nor a salesman for God. God does not need anyone to defend His case. His case was settled long ago on the cross of Calvary. God does not need anyone to sell His Gospel. His Gospel is free without charge to anyone who will hear and believe. What God wants is for a nobody to go and preach His Word. You and I are to speak and guide people to Jesus and permit God to win souls unto Himself no matter what we are doing.

We can witness to people just about any time and anywhere. We Christians are a witness of the Lord Jesus and therefore we can soulwin through witnessing. When Jesus becomes your personal Savior, you automatically become qualified with the Holy Spirit's inner dwelling stamp of approval to be a witness on Christ's behalf. Therefore, as a witness you have the responsibility to testify unto people what you know about the man CHRIST JESUS to the nonbelievers who put Him in question (1 Peter 3:15). What an awesome privilege! But some baby Christians might say, "I don't know anything about Jesus just yet." And I say, "That's not true." You know that He is the Savior and you know that He saved you! You can and should testify to the lost about your personal experiences with Jesus, such as what Jesus has done for and in you.

Another good reason why you are to testify about your personal experiences is that there are many times in life when you cannot pull out the Holy Bible with someone, such as at work. Your personal testimony, just as the Word of God, is evidence. You can use that to present the evidence that they are lost and have a need for the Savoir Jesus Christ (Revelation 12:11). The Word of God certainly does stand alone in convicting someone but in the many times when you do not have the Bible you ought to use your powerful personal stories as evidence. You, as a witness, can use your stories because you have encountered the Savior, and you absolutely know what Jesus Christ has done for you. Additionally, no one is able to refute your testimony of who you have met and who you know.

The Bible reveals to us in John 6:29 that soulwinning is God's work to bring a lost, unbelieving sinner to believe on Jesus Christ for salvation. The term "soulwinning" simply refers to the practice of attempting to guide lost sinners to the Lord Jesus Christ for salvation and then continuing to direct them closer to the Savior through discipleship. It is our Supreme Duty to do so. He saved us, and the outcome, or the result of our love and appreciation for Him, is to reach out to mankind and assist in guiding them closer to God (1 John 2:33). Indisputably, you and I cannot save anybody—only Jesus Christ can save! And the God of all time and all space will save anybody who believes on the Lord Jesus Christ!!! More interestingly to know is that God Almighty desires all Christians, yes ALL CHRISTIANS, to be active soulwinners in their daily lives. Soulwinning is NOT only for pastors, missionaries, or evangelists. I repeat this statement because the Bible repeats the point that soulwinning is NOT only for pastors, missionaries, and evangelists. On the contrary, the excellent good news is that God entrusts the wonderful responsibility of soulwinning to ALL disciples of Jesus Christ. This includes clergymen as well as the laymen. God makes this very clear in 1 Thessalonians 2:4. The verse reads: *"But as we were allowed of God to be put in trust with the gospel, even so we speak; not as pleasing men, but God, which trieth our hearts."* This passage of scripture teaches us that God entrusts us, all of us, with His Gospel. He does not entrust His Gospel with the angels or with the cherubim, nor any of the millions of other species that exists on this planet and maybe out in the heavens. More amazingly, God chooses to use human beings. If you are a saved, born-again believer, then you are an authorized agent of the Lord, and you are COMMANDED to be a soulwinner. Since you are commanded, God has already gifted you with ALL the abilities that you need to accomplish His work of soulwinning. Listen to the clear instructions of Jesus Christ in Matthew 28:19 and 20, *"Go ye therefore, and teach all nations, baptizing them in the name of the Father, and of the Son, and of the Holy Ghost: Teaching them to observe all things whatsoever I have commanded you: and, lo, I am with you alway, even unto the end of the world. Amen."* Again, as I mentioned earlier, it is our responsibility and it is our extraordinary privilege as the children of God to *"teach them."* Go out, get involved in people's lives, and guide them to Jesus Christ through the opening of our mouths and telling them the good news.

So then, the next question that arises in one's mind is, "Who are we to teach?" We are to teach the Gospel of Christ to lost sinners. We are to explain to them that God has given us His Law for us to live by and we should assist them to understand that they have broken the Law of God. We are to teach them that they are guilty before God and that He ultimately will hold them accountable and judge them at the end of their lives on account of their transgressions in accordance to His Law. We are to teach them about God the Son—Christ Jesus. How He came to this Earth. How He lived a perfect life without breaking one command of God's Law. How He paid the punishment of death by gruesomely being vicariously sacrificed on a cross for our sins. Then we are to teach them that He was buried and that on the third day He literally and physically resurrected from the dead and now sits at the right hand of the throne of God. Then we need to tell them that Jesus is now urging sinners, like themselves, to believe on Him and to receive Him as their personal Savior.

We are to teach those whom we lead to Christ how they can continue to get to know God in a deep, meaningful way and how they, too, need to get involved in other's lives and effectively win others to Christ. What a thrill and a joy it is to proclaim the Gospel of Jesus Christ and to be involved in people's lives! How greedy and selfish it would be for us to withhold this treasure from new converts and impede them from learning that they, too, can be part in the joyous, awesome work of soulwinning. Just as it was the responsibility of the disciples in Jesus' day to teach the Gospel to all nations (all people), it is our responsibility to do the same today. In the disciples' time, when someone became a believer, accepting Jesus Christ as their personal Savior, they were to help that new convert grow in the Lord and become a soulwinner too. This is God's divine plan to win the lost to Christ—we are responsible!!!

I must say that sin is no trifle. It is not taken lightly in the sight of God. The God-inspired work of soulwinning takes an enormous effort. It takes the combined efforts of the Triune God to keep someone out of Hell—God the Father to provide the plan of salvation, God the Holy Spirit to convict, and God the Son, Jesus Christ, to redeem an individual through His blood. The saved believer's part is to go and tell the lost sinner. The unsaved individual is to believe, repent, and accept the gift of eternal life. In other words....

God the Father's Part — PROVIDE the plan of salvation
God the Holy Spirit's Part — CONVICT the people of their sins
God the Son's Part — REDEEM the people through His blood
Christian's Part — GO and TELL the people
Lost Sinner's Part — BELIEVE on the Lord Jesus Christ

CHAPTER 3

What Is the Gospel of Jesus Christ?

For I am not ashamed of the gospel of Christ: for it is the power of God unto salvation to every one that believeth; to the Jew first, and also to the Greek.
– Romans 1:16

Okay, I understand that you might be thinking, "Isn't it obvious what the Gospel of Jesus Christ is?" And sure, I can respond to your assumption that yes it should be obvious to every "Christian" what the Gospel of Jesus Christ is. But, maybe, to your bewilderment, the answer is that there are many so-called "Christians" today that do not know what the Gospel of Jesus Christ is. For that reason, I have written and included this chapter into this book. From personal experience, I have run into hundreds of "Christians" who have given me a wrong explanation of what the Gospel of Jesus Christ is when I have asked them what it is. I have heard so many wrong explanations that it is just pitiful. So many so-called "Christians" have not answered correctly, and many of these responders have been nowhere close to what the Bible says is the Gospel of Jesus Christ. Now, I am not saying that all Christians do not know what the Gospel is. I am simply stating the fact that numerous amounts of so-called "saved" people do not know what the Bible says it is. Even worse, is that if someone does not know what the Gospel of Jesus Christ is, then I question if the individual really is saved or not. Remember the Bible teaches all believers to *"Examine yourselves, whether ye be in the faith; prove your own selves"* in 2 Corinthians 13:5. That means we are to examine our personal beliefs and convictions to see if they align with the Word of God. If someone's personal beliefs or convictions on any particular matter does not line up according to what the Bible says, then that individual is in the wrong. Second Corinthians 13:5 indirectly is saying that just because an individual calls himself a Christian does not entitle him to the privilege of being a Christian. In the same way, just because you loyally attend baseball games does not privilege you to be a televised sports reporter or one of the players.

Nonetheless, I am not God, so I cannot and will not judge on who is and who is not a Christian. I leave that up to God. It is neither my duty nor my worry to try to figure out who really is a child of God and who deceivingly is not a child of God (Matthew 13:24-30). That's God's job, thankfully! My duty, just as it is your duty, is to urge people to examine themselves and prove if their faith is genuine or if they are fooling themselves.

Another point is that nobody can be a soulwinner if he does not know what the Gospel of Jesus Christ is. Sure, you can pass out tracts, and maybe a few people will get saved that way. However, that just means you are a Gospel tract distributor. I say hallelujah for folks that do that, and by no means stop passing out tracts! But, if you want to be a true soulwinner, an effective soulwinner, one who is sharp and effective in the work, then you first have to know the Gospel of Jesus Christ. It does not matter how eloquent an individual can speak or how sincere he is in his efforts. If an individual does not know what the Gospel is, then he simply is like the religious leaders that Jesus warned about in Mathew 15:14. Jesus sternly warned about individuals who are blind from the truth, because these same blind people lead other blind people farther away from the truth and down into a ditch of destruction. If you cannot simply direct people only to Jesus Christ, then you are presently useless for the Kingdom of God. You will be found to be like those religious leaders of Jesus' day who took prey of the lost and made their way to Hell even more arduous. May we not be found leading someone from one lost way into another lost way absent from God! What a horrible day of judgment that is going to be for such wicked individuals.

With all of that said, then what is the Gospel of Jesus Christ? Let's break this simple truth down by first looking at the word "gospel." According to the Wikipedia Free Encyclopedia, the word gospel derives from the Old English word, gōd-spell (rarely godspel), which means "good tidings" or "glad tidings." So today's modern English word gospel simply translates to mean good news. The opposite of good news is bad news. Therefore, the correct news about Jesus Christ is good news. If you do not direct someone to Jesus, then you are not giving him good news. Instead, you are giving him more bad news.

For a quick and brief side note about the understanding of "gospel" in the Holy Bible, I would like to make mention the next few statements about "gospel". The Bible is filled with not just one, but with many gospels, much good news concerning truths: such as, the "gospel" of the Kingdom, the "gospel" of the grace of God, and the "gospel" of the glory of Christ, and so forth. If you would do a thorough topical study on the subject of "gospel" in the Holy Bible, you would learn that some theologians go as far as to state that there are at least eight gospels in the Holy Bible. Then there are the writings of holy men chosen by God to write the Gospel of Matthew, the Gospel of Mark, the Gospel of Luke, and the Gospel of John. And all four of these Gospel book writings centralize around the one and true Gospel of Jesus Christ; which is the only One Gospel that is able to convert a soul unto repentance and save individuals from the judgment of God (Psalm 19:7). The Gospel of Jesus Christ is the Good News that Jesus Christ has made salvation available to all people through His death and resurrection; not only to the Jews but to all kindred's, tongues, and nations of all people.

As we examine history, we will come to a realization that God has always declared His Gospel (good news) to mankind throughout the ages. Even before God came down in human flesh to save us on the cross, He declared His Gospel through the prophecies of many holy men of God. These men of God were known as or called prophets, because, in simple explanation, they were by God allowed to publicly proclaim His Word to the people around them. Some of the many prophets that God rose up to proclaim and prophecy His Gospel were holy and devout men such as the Prophet Moses. Others included holy men such as the Prophet Jeremiah, the Prophet Micah, the Prophet Daniel, the Prophet Isaiah, and the Prophet Zechariah. Of course, there were numerous others, but one particular prophet of great interest was the Prophet Isaiah. For time's sake within this book, I will only touch on some of the prophecies given through the Prophet Isaiah in relation to the Gospel of Jesus Christ. However, I would encourage you to go study your Bible in greater depth to familiarize yourself with the scores of other prophecies written by many other prophets found in the Old Testament of the Holy Bible. Or purchase my book, *IMPORTANT SOULWINNING VERSES of the Holy Bible's Fundamental Doctrines*, and then study the last two chapters where I provide you with almost 500 Messianic prophecies and their New Testament fulfillments.

God used the Prophet Isaiah to speak and pen down in detail prophetic revelation about the Gospel of Jesus Christ to the people of His time, informing them of what God would eventually do to establish the way for forgiveness of sins and eternal salvation for all generations of time past, present, and the future.

Praise be to God! You and I today have the privilege to read the Prophet Isaiah's writings. We learn about what the people of his day heard him teach about concerning the Gospel of the coming Messiah, the Lord Jesus Christ, and the many details relating to His life in this world. For example, he prophesied that the Gospel would be established through a virgin. The scripture text, Isaiah 7:14, prophetically exposes: *"Therefore the Lord himself will give you a sign; Behold, a virgin shall conceive and bear a Son, and shall call His name Immanuel."* The word

Immanuel is the Hebrew title meaning "God with us." It is important to remember that within the Israelite Jewish cultural names were more than just an appellation used within a society to merely distinguish one person from other people, as in our modern day society; a name was given to a baby to descriptively depict God's intentions for the person's life. God magnificently described one entity of Himself through the name Immanuel. It was also not unusual for a person throughout their life to beget several names. It was the Jewish custom of those days to rename someone who had experienced a life-changing event. For example, Abram became Abraham. Saul became Paul. Simon or Cephas became Peter. Each of these men in the Holy Bible experienced a life-changing event and one result of that experience is that the Lord transformed their hearts and revolutionized their names. So, as we see, it was not unusual at all for God to have the name Immanuel and also Yeshua or more commonly known in English as Jesus.

Then in Isaiah 9:6-7, God prophesied through the Prophet Isaiah about what shall come about with this Gospel of Jesus. This scripture text prophetically declares, *"For unto us a child is born, unto us a son is given: and the government shall be upon his shoulder: and his name shall be called Wonderful, Counsellor, The mighty God, The everlasting Father, The Prince of Peace. Of the increase of his government and peace there shall be no end, upon the throne of David, and upon his kingdom, to order it, and to establish it with judgment and with justice from henceforth even for ever. The zeal of the LORD of hosts will perform this."*

God was not done just yet prophetically explaining the Gospel of Jesus Christ through the Prophet Isaiah. God continued to inform mankind about how this Savior would be a servant who would suffer much for the sins of mankind. Isaiah 52:13-15 prophetically explains, *"Behold, my servant shall deal prudently, he shall be exalted and extolled, and be very high. As many were astonied at thee; his visage was so marred more than any man, and his form more than the sons of men: So shall he sprinkle many nations; the kings shall shut their mouths at him: for that which had not been told them shall they see; and that which they had not heard shall they consider."*

Again, God used the Prophet Isaiah to prophetically describe in details to us how the life of this Servant, Jesus, would suffer a great deal for the sins of humanity, and His sufferings would present the opportunity for mankind to be saved from their sins. Isaiah 53:1-12 prophetically details, *"Who hath believed our report? and to whom is the arm of the LORD revealed? For he shall grow up before him as a tender plant, and as a root out of a dry ground: he hath no form nor comeliness; and when we shall see him, there is no beauty that we should desire him. He is despised and rejected of men; a man of sorrows, and acquainted with grief: and we hid as it were our faces from him; he was despised, and we esteemed him not. Surely he hath borne our griefs, and carried our sorrows: yet we did esteem him stricken, smitten of God, and afflicted. But he was wounded for our transgressions, he was bruised for our iniquities: the chastisement of our peace was upon him; and with his stripes we are healed. All we like sheep have gone astray; we have turned every one to his own way; and the LORD hath laid on him the iniquity of us all. He was oppressed, and he was afflicted, yet he opened not his mouth: he is brought as a lamb to the slaughter, and as a sheep before her shearers is dumb, so he openeth not his mouth. He was taken from prison and from judgment: and who shall declare his generation? for he was cut off out of the land of the living: for the transgression of my people was he stricken. And he made his grave with the wicked, and with the rich in his death; because he had done no violence, neither was any deceit in his mouth. Yet it pleased the LORD to bruise him; he hath put him to grief: when thou shalt make his soul an offering for sin, he shall see his seed, he shall prolong his days, and the pleasure of the LORD shall prosper in his hand. He shall see of the travail of his soul, and shall be satisfied: by his knowledge shall my righteous servant justify many; for he shall bear their iniquities. Therefore will I divide him a portion with the great, and he shall divide the spoil with the strong; because he hath poured out his soul unto death: and he was numbered with the transgressors; and he bare the sin of many, and made intercession for the transgressors."*

Isn't it amazing that God revealed in exact details the Gospel of Jesus Christ to generations hundreds and hundreds of years before Jesus would ever place a foot on this earth? Nonetheless, just as God clearly declared this Gospel through extensive prophecies in the Old Testament, He also has declared unto us the Gospel in the New Testament through many scriptures. Over 400 times our Holy Bible declares that Jesus is the only way for salvation. Over 700 times our Holy Bible declares that it is the blood that redeems us for salvation. Out of all these verses, one particular passage of scripture in the New Testament that surely stands out above all these other verses is the verse where the Apostle Paul explained in detail what the Gospel of Jesus Christ is. In 1 Corinthians 15:1-8, he wrote, *"Moreover, brethren, I declare unto you the gospel which I preached unto you, which also ye have received, and wherein ye stand; By which also ye are saved,…... <u>how that Christ died for our sins according to the scriptures; And that He was buried, and that He rose again the third day according to the scriptures</u>: And that he was seen of Cephas* [Peter], *then of the twelve: After that, He was seen of above five hundred brethren at once; of whom the greater part remain unto this present, but some are fallen asleep. After that, He was seen of James; then of all the apostles. And last of all He was seen of me also…"* Paul plainly put it in verses 3 and 4 that the Gospel of Jesus Christ is none other than the death, burial, and resurrection of Jesus Christ. PLEASE NOTE and make attention to this—It is not just one or two of these aspects of Christ's events. The Gospel of Jesus Christ in its entirety is all three events. Without the mention of all three events, the death, burial and the resurrection, the Gospel is not clearly and fully being portrayed and we are doing a disservice to not mention all three.

Now that we see the Gospel in some of the writings of both the Old and the New Testaments of the Bible, let's look at the application of the Gospel of Jesus. If we are to be a soulwinner we must know the whole Gospel of Jesus Christ, but we must also understand its implications. We must be able to present the Gospel with simplicity. For the Gospel is simple (2 Corinthians 11:3). It is so simple that even a little child can understand it and believe on the Lord Jesus for salvation. We must be able to point people to Jesus. We are not to direct them to ourselves nor to manmade traditions or rules, but we are to direct them only to Jesus Christ! For example, one passage of scripture in the Gospel of John depicts a story where two people pointed other individuals to Jesus. The first person of interest was John. John had been discipling some young men, and when they happened to come into the presence of Jesus, John immediately directed his disciples' attention off himself and pointed them to Jesus. Later on, one of those same disciples, Andrew, pointed his brother Simon Peter to Jesus. The implication is that we too must do the same and point people to the Savior Jesus Christ. We read about their story in John 1:35-42. The passage reads: *"Again the next day after John stood, and two of his disciples; And looking upon Jesus as he walked, he saith, Behold the Lamb of God! And the two disciples heard him speak, and they followed Jesus. Then Jesus turned, and saw them following, and saith unto them, What seek ye? They said unto him, Rabbi, (which is to say, being interpreted, Master,) where dwellest thou? He saith unto them, Come and see. They came and saw where he dwelt, and abode with him that day: for it was about the tenth hour. One of the two which heard John speak, and followed him, was Andrew, Simon Peter's brother. He first findeth his own brother Simon, and saith unto him, We have found the Messias, which is, being interpreted, the Christ. And he brought him to Jesus. And when Jesus beheld him, he said, Thou art Simon the son of Jona: thou shalt be called Cephas, which is by interpretation, A stone."*

We see that Andrew was following a wise man, John the Baptist. But when Andrew was pointed to Jesus, Andrew came to the realization that it was Jesus whom he must follow, not another man. Andrew, Simon Peter's brother, made the decision in his personal life to choose to follow Christ at that moment. Andrew realized that his own brother, Simon Peter, needed to be saved as well. Andrew soon went to his brother, filled with enthusiasm, and exclaimed that he had found the Christ. He had gotten saved! He then proceeded to bring Simon Peter to Jesus.

I don't know about you, but that, in my eyes, is such a beautiful picture of what we are to be doing. In this passage of scripture, we learn some practical principles that a Christian must implement into his life if he is going to be a soulwinner, as Andrew was quickly learning to be. The first principle is that we Christians need to be filled with enthusiasm because we too have found the wonderful Savior. We have no reason to be moping around with sadness and filled with gloom and doom. We have the Savior. We have life and life eternal! If there is no other reason to be joyful in life, it is that we are joined together with the Savior and have eternal life.

A second principle we learn from this passage is that we need to choose and actively go to people and point them to Jesus. Just as Andrew pointed his brother to Jesus, his brother Simon Peter was able to be saved. We too need to actively and purposefully go out, tell people the Gospel and lead them to Jesus to be saved. As a result of Peter's salvation, he eventually became one of the greatest preachers of his day and literally thousands of people came to Jesus Christ because of his being used of God! Not only that, but beyond his imagination, God has used his testimony and his writings to reach around 2,000 years of generations with the Gospel of Jesus Christ. Today, God wants to use you and I to point people to Jesus so that they too can become great, mighty individuals of God. We never know what God is going to do with a "nobody" to whom we preach the Gospel. We just might be walking over and telling the Gospel to another future mighty man of God, like Peter.

Therefore, the main principle of the passage that we need to apply within our lives is that we need to point people to Jesus Christ. It is a shame, but most professing Christians do not know how to lead someone to Jesus. And it is a wonder why so many do not understand why they do not have any real joy in their lives. It breaks God's heart and it is a devastating shame.

In the Gospel of Jesus Christ there are only three major truths: His death for sin, burial and victorious resurrection. It is very beneficial to compel lost sinners to come to a realization of these three. It is also beneficial to compel lost sinners to understand four other truths which circulate around the Gospel truth. Those seven truths are as follows:

— 1st Point —
A Person Can Know for Sure That He Can Go to Heaven and Have Eternal Life

The Bible speaks with certainty that you can know for sure where you are going to spend your eternity. The Holy Bible promises us in 1 John 5:13: *"These things have I written unto you that believe on the name of the Son of God; that ye may know that ye have eternal life."* If it is in the Bible then it definitely is true. Jesus is offering eternal life to anyone who will accept it. As a soulwinner, we must ask directly in love and not play around with the question concerning salvation. We must just ask people plainly, "If you were to die today, do you know for sure, are you 100% confident and certain, that you would go to Heaven, or do you have some doubt?" This way we can quickly find out if they are on their way to Heaven or Hell. If you ask them with love and not with judgment, they will give you an answer. Their answer will inform us of where to take them next.

There are more encouraging words and promises from the Bible that we can tell them to ensure them that they can have eternal life. A verse in John 1:12 says, *"But as many as received Him, to them gave he power to become the sons of God, even to them that believe on his name."* The Apostle Paul also wrote in Titus 1:2: *"In hope of eternal life, which God, that cannot lie, promised before the world began."* Hope in the Bible is not what we define it as today. Today's hope that we throw around all the time in our common speech is filled with uncertainty. However, the hope being spoken of in this verse is a sure thing that you can place your complete confidence in. It is not uncertain. It is an absolute. Bible hope is not what we "think" we will get, but rather, what we "know" we will receive because of God's faithful promises! And one great promise God gives is that, though we do not deserve it, we certainly can be sure that we can have eternal life! For John 3:16 promises, *"For God so loved the world, that he gave his only begotten Son, that whosoever believeth in him should not perish, but have everlasting life."*

— 2ⁿᵈ Point —
A Person Must Realize That He Is a Sinner

This is the foremost important point of the Gospel of Jesus Christ as a whole, and I must add that it is the most difficult part for many people to come to understand and realize. Before someone can understand or appreciate the good news, he or she needs to hear and understand the bad news first. Yes, the Gospel contains bad news. But for a glorious reason it is utmost vitally important that a person must understand the bad news: that he is a sinner. For God has commanded each and every single one of us in 1 Peter 1:16 to *"be ye holy; for I* [God] *am holy."* God has a standard and His standard is holiness. His standard of holiness can be measured by His perfect Law—The Ten Commandments. Romans 7:12 says, *"Wherefore the law is holy, and the commandment holy, and just, and good."* First John 3:4 informs us that a sinner is someone who has transgressed the Law of God. Meaning, they have disobeyed and they have acted against what God deems right to do. When someone violates just one of God's commandments it makes him a lawbreaker, a transgressor of the Law (1 John 3:4). James 2:10 notifies us that *"For whosoever shall keep the whole law, and yet offend in one point, he is guilty of all."* Yes, it just takes only one sin to make us a sinner before the righteous, holy eyes of God. Nonetheless, the reality is that you and I are indeed guilty of committing sin, and certainly many, Many, MANY more sins than just one!

The Bible, especially in the book of Romans, is filled with many verses about the topic of our sin state. Here are just a few verses out of many that I personally use when talking to people about this important point of the Gospel. The Bible in Romans 3:10 declares, *"As it is written, There is none righteous, no, not one."* All of us are born with a sin nature that is against God. Some of us are just more disobedient than others, but all of us are sinners. The Bible informs us in great detail that we are sinners indeed. Romans 3:23 declares, *"For all have sinned, and come short of the glory of God."* We need to show our hearer that God's standard is perfection. However, we all have fallen short of God's perfection. And, we have a major problem—we are rotten lawbreaking sinners, and come short of His perfect standard!

The Bible says in 1 Samuel 16:7: *"[F]or the LORD seeth not as man seeth; for man looketh on the outward appearance, but the LORD looketh on the heart."* Though our friends, family, and acquaintances might have many good comments about us, God looks upon our hearts and He sees us as sinners through and through. He looks upon us and sees who we really are. We are none other than filthy and old, crumbled up, dry individuals (Isaiah 64:6). For God sees that we are a sinner by birth—for Psalm 58:3 says, *"The wicked are estranged from the womb: they go astray as soon as they be born, speaking lies."* He sees that we are sinners by nature—for Jeremiah 17:9 says, *"The heart is deceitful above all things, and desperately wicked: who can know it?"* He sees that we are sinners by deed—for James 4:17 says, *"Therefore to him that knoweth to do good, and doeth it not, to him it is sin."* And He sees that we are sinners by choice—for John 3:19 declares, *"And this is the condemnation, that light is come into the world, and men loved darkness rather than light, because their deeds were evil."*

If one needs more scriptures to comprehend our sin condition, one can look at verses such as Romans 1:28-32, Romans 3:9, Romans 3:19, Romans 3:11-12, Romans 5:8, Romans 5:12, and Romans 11:32. Romans 3:9-20 repeatedly affirms that we are sinners—that, in fact, our entire beings are tainted with evil. Some of my personal favorite verses which declare our sin condition are Ecclesiastes 7:20, Galatians 3:22 and 1 John 1:8-10. Ecclesiastes 7:20 states: *"For there is not a just man upon earth, that doeth good, and sinneth not."* Galatians 3:22 says, *"But the scripture hath concluded all under sin, that the promise by faith of Jesus Christ might be given to them that believe."* Last, 1 John 1:8-10 says, *"If we say that we have no sin, we deceive ourselves, and the truth is not in us. If we confess our sins, he is faithful and just to forgive us our sins, and to cleanse us from all unrighteousness. If we say that we have not sinned, we make him a liar, and his word is not in us."*

The Bible concludes that an individual must realize and believe that he is a sinner before he can be saved. It must not merely be an intellectual unremorseful belief of "yeah, I'm a sinner, so what do I do next." A person must have a heartfelt understanding and conviction that he has offended God through the breaking of His Law and that he has a seriously big problem—he is a sinner! If someone does not believe he is a sinner then he cannot be saved. Until a person realizes that he is a sinner and that he is doomed, the Cross of Jesus Christ is a farce to him. If someone does not know he is a sinner then he cannot be saved. Conviction of sin always brings a fearful binding sense of the Law, it makes a person hopeless. This is why there is not any other reason to come to Christ than for the reason that you are desperately convicted that your sins have separated you from your Creator and Judge (Isaiah 59:2), and you need reconciliation with Him (Colossians 1:20). This is the reason why even in the church today, there are many faithful church attendees who are on their way to Hell. They have come to Christ for the wrong reason. If someone comes to Christ for any other reason than to receive help for their wretched sins, then he cannot get saved. Until someone sees that he has a horrible sin condition, that he is a sinner, he cannot even call upon the name of Jesus for salvation to save him from his sins, for he will not, until he realizes it.

I strongly encourage you to really nail this point down with someone. Do it with love of course, but do it. Make sure they are convinced and convicted of their sins, or you will dangerously lead them through man's traditional replications of a religious exercise instead of a true repentance. God is not looking for a replication of His work. God is looking for a genuine repentance.

I can remember many times where I have worked with a number of people and stayed on this one topic, that they are sinners, for a long time until I seen the conviction in their eyes. Now, I would like to interrupt and say that for some, that long time was hours, but for others it has been weeks. When I finally saw the conviction, they were then ready and almost begging to hear what the answer is for their sin. This is what saves someone. Someone is saved when they call upon Jesus for HELP for their guilt. And oh, we would do much more help for this world if we would just take our time and proclaim the Gospel, that people are guilty sinners. It would do so much more good for people to come to the conclusion that they are guilty sinners and in need of a Savior than this ecumenical lie that we come to Jesus for all our wants, desires, requests, and likes, as if He is some Santa Clause or something. Some of these might be good, but none of them are THE reason to come to Jesus.

We need to preach the old-fashioned declaration that we are guilty sinners and we are in need of the Savior! When people understand they are sinners, then their heart is ripe to search for the answer for their guilt. Then people are willing to listen about why Jesus came and what their response must be. We cannot do anything to appease God, except to call out with conviction that we really need Him.

— 3rd Point —
A Person Must Realize That Sin Must Be Paid For

Romans 6:23 informs us: *"For the wages of sin is death; but the gift of God is eternal life through Jesus Christ our Lord."* They need to understand that sin cannot be forgiven but we sinners can be forgiven. The truth is that sin must be paid for! It might be a helpful idea to explain to them that the word "wage" means earnings or payments. Therefore, the Bible is telling us that every single time we disobey God (sinning), we are actually earning the penalty of death. For example, you may want to explain this point by first opening up with the story of Adam and Eve. The entrance of sin into God's perfect creation brought immediate spiritual death and started the ticking of the clock to their ultimate physical death. Genesis 3:8 says, *"[Adam] and his wife hid themselves from the presence of the LORD God..."* Just a few verses before they were engaged in a perfect, wonderful relationship with God. Now they were hiding from Him. Isn't that peculiar! Why would you hide from your best friend? The answer is because they disobeyed God's commandment. Their disobedience brought the horrible experience of immediate spiritual death and therefore their exposure to sin afforded them shame and to not want to be in His holy presence. Consequently, they reacted as any sinner does—they went hiding from God, or at least they tried to hide from Him, and to think they tried to hide from the God that loved them. Later on, Genesis 3:19 reveals to us how they began to experience the physical death. God is speaking in the verse and He said unto them: *"In the sweat of thy face shalt thou eat bread, til thou return unto the ground; for out of it was thou taken: for dust thou art, and unto dust shalt thou return."*

There is also one more death. Sin also condemns man to an eternal death—the awfulness of being separated from God for all eternity—forever! The Holy Bible reveals in Hebrews 9:27 that *"it is appointed unto men once to die, but after this the judgment."* This judgment is not one to see if your "good" outweighs your "bad," for there can be no sin in Heaven, not even just one! Revelation 21:27 informs us that: *"And there shall in no wise enter into it* [the Heavenly city] *any thing that defileth, neither whatsoever worketh abomination, or maketh a lie: but they which are written in the Lamb's book of life."* Judgment Day offers no hope for anyone! The only hope of Judgment Day is eternal condemnation, for Revelation 20:11-15 promises that: *"And I saw a great white throne, and him that sat on it, from whose face the earth and the heaven fled away; and there was found no place for them. And I saw the dead, small and great stand before God; and the books were opened: and another book was opened, which is the book of life: and the dead were judged out of those things which were written in the books, according to their works... and they were judged every man according to their works. And death and hell were cast into the lake of fire. This is the second death. And whosoever was not found written in the book of life was cast into the lake of fire."*

You will want to explain to a lost soul that just as the Bible informs us in Revelation 20:11-15 that there is an eternal death of separation from God in a place called the lake of fire, all deserve to go there who have sinned because they earn their way there and they deserve to be there. So, just as you receive wages from your employer, there must be a payment made for your sins, too. Henceforth, because one sins, his sins have afforded him the earning of Hell.

— 4th Point —
A Person Must Realize That He Cannot Do Anything to Work off His Sin Debt

Once someone understands that he is on his way to Hell and deserves to go there because he has disobeyed God, he might start to think that perhaps there is something that he can do to pay off his sin debt. Most people consider and believe this lie. We soulwinners must show lost souls that no one can pay nor do anything to work off their sin debt. The Bible says in Psalm 49:7-8: *"None of them can by any means redeem his brother, nor give to God a ransom for him: (For the redemption of their soul is precious, and it ceaseth for ever:)."* This is a straight-forward passage. Let's look at some of the words in these two verses. The words "to redeem" according to the Noah Webster 1828 Dictionary means to purchase back. The words "to give to God," well, we all know what it means to give. The Noah Webster 1828 Dictionary defines a "ransom" as the money or price paid for the redemption of a prisoner, slave, or servant. Romans chapter 6 explicitly lets us know that apart from Christ, people are helpless, poor servants to sin. Again, Psalm 49:7-8 lets us know that *"None of them can by any means redeem his brother, nor give to God a ransom for him: (For the redemption of their soul is precious, and it ceaseth for ever:)."* So accordingly, if none of us are able to purchase, buy, redeem, or give to God anything, not even a ransom, such as money or things to purchase salvation for a human brother on this earth, it makes total sense that none of us can purchase our own salvation. Jesus clarified the reason behind this; In

Matthew 5:3 he informed us that we are poor. We are so poor that we are more or less spiritually bankrupt. There is no way at all that we could or can ever afford to give God anything for the purchase of our salvation or the purchase of anyone else's salvation. We are so in debt with God that not only do we lack the sufficiency to pay Him for our salvation; we can never do enough work to pay off the enormity of our debt unto Him. We cannot work or pay for our salvation. The reason is explained in Ephesians 2:8-9. It says, *"For by grace are ye saved through faith; and that not of yourselves: it is the gift of God: Not of works, lest any man should boast."* Then Titus 3:5 explains that *"Not by works of righteousness which we have done, but according to his mercy he saved us, by the washing of regeneration, and renewing of the Holy Ghost."* Even the smallest percentage of works debases saving grace, as Romans 11:6 makes so pointedly clear: *"And if by grace, then is it no more of works: otherwise grace is no more grace. But if it be of works, then is it no more grace."*

As you talk with a nonbeliever about this important point you can show them that even Adam and Eve could not pay for their sins, and since them, all of humankind has become indebted to God with the same large debt of sin. You can show your hearer Romans 5:12, which says, *"Wherefore, as by one man sin entered into the world, and death by sin; and so death passed upon all men, for that all have sinned."* Show your hearer that after Adam and Eve disobeyed God, they became separated from God because of their sins, and they eventually died physically for their sin. Then you can compare us to that of Adam and Eve. You can show them from Isaiah 59:2 that our sins separate us from God too. This separation is an enormous chasm that we can never fill. Isaiah 59:2 informs us that *"But your iniquities have separated between you and your God."* You might want to even show them Luke 16:19-31, which tells us the true story of an unsaved rich man who went to Hell, and a saved man named Lazarus who went to Heaven. The rich man rejected the Gospel while living here on earth. He died and went to Hell to pay for his sins. In Hell he lifted up his eyes in torment and repented that he ever rejected God's calling here on earth. But it was and is now too late. He and anyone else who goes to Hell will spend an eternity to pay back their sin debt to God. That is very sad, because once a person is in Hell, it is too late to repent for salvation. Sin separates people from God, and if one does not repent on this earth in this lifetime, it is going to take a whole eternity to pay God the retribution that is due to Him for their sin debt.

Sometimes a great verse to show nonbelievers is Revelation 20:15. You should show them from this verse that the unsaved sinner's sins will eternally separate them in the everlasting punishment of the lake of fire. Revelation 20:15 says, "*And whosoever was not found written in the book of life was cast into the lake of fire.*"

Furthermore, there is absolutely nothing we can do to pay off our debt because there is no way we can change ourselves. We are deeply blotted with a dirty sin stain and though we try to clean ourselves or do something to work for salvation, there is nothing we can do to clean the sin off ourselves or our record. God declares to us in Isaiah 64:6: "*But we are all as an unclean thing, and all our righteousnesses* [good deeds in life] *are as filthy rags; and we all do fade as a leaf; and our iniquities, like the wind, have taken us away.*" Just as Jeremiah 13:23 brings us to the point of understanding that as an Ethiopian cannot change his skin or the leopard his spots, nor can we change our sin state that we are overwhelmed in. We are so stained with sin that working to try to earn salvation is like an oil-covered bird trying to lick off a manmade oil spill that he is drenched in. It is impossible. But what is impossible with man, God has made a way possible through Himself. Though it is impossible for man to save himself, God has still made it possible for man to receive salvation.

— 5th Point —
A Person Must Believe That Jesus
Paid the Penalty for His Guilty Sins

As I just mentioned in the last sentence of the previous point, it is impossible for man to work his way for salvation. Though it is impossible with man, God has done the impossible and made a way for us to able to receive salvation. The previous points were all the bad news of the Gospel of Jesus Christ—that people are sinners, lost, and facing a Christless eternity without any hope! But hallelujah and thank God for the good news, which is only made possible through God Himself. The good news is that Jesus Christ died for our sins. The truth must be recognized; Though God loves us humans, He hates our wickedness! He cannot and He will not overlook or excuse even one of our sins, because He is just. God's justice demands that sin be paid for. It would be unjust of God to overlook and excuse sin and not allow it to be judged. God is just and therefore He will judge and punish sinful men on the account of their wicked deeds in the future.

Yet, God desires so much to bring people into a personal relationship with Himself. God knows the future of that awful Day of Judgment and He presently desires to rescue people from having to go to the Great White Throne Judgment. For He knows how sin separates people from Him and He knows that the awful punishment of eternal separation from Him is in a place called the lake of fire for those people who choose to attend the Great Judgment. Nonetheless, sin must be paid for and someone will always have to pay for sins. Therefore, He designed a way for our sins to be paid for so that justice can be appeased and man can stand in a righteous relationship with God. So, here's the good news! God's righteousness, justice, and love have met and are satisfied in Christ Jesus.

First Peter 3:18 lets us know that "[*Christ*] *also hath once suffered for sins, the just for the unjust, that he might bring us to God.*" Romans 5:8 reveals the way God created for our sins to be judged and punished, and that was through the death punishment of Jesus Christ. The voluminous verse reads: "*But God commendeth his love toward us, in that, while we were yet sinners, Christ died for us.*" The word commendeth is an old English word for the modern English word to demonstrate or to show. Therefore, God demonstrates His love toward us that He allowed His Son Jesus to pay the penalty (guilt) of man's sin. The Son of God bore no sin of His own. He is "*holy, harmless, undefiled, separate from sinners,*" according to Hebrews 7:26. First Peter 2:22 lets us know that Jesus "*did no sin.*" And I like the words "*while we were yet sinners*" in Romans 5:8—implying that God will never wait for us to get our act together, because we cannot. We are stained with sin, and therefore God took care of our sin through the death of His Son without our help, assistance, or work.

Romans 6:23 informs us that sin has a price on it: "*For the wages of sin is death.*" Romans 5:8 says that Jesus paid that price: "*...Christ died for us...*" You might want to tell the lost sinner again that we personally owe a debt that we never can repay. But Jesus paid that debt that He did not owe. As Jesus hung upon the cross, 2 Corinthians 5:21 tells us that God the Father literally "*hath made Him* [Jesus] *to be sin for us, who knew no sin; that we might be made the righteousness of God in Him.*" Then 1 Peter 3:18 reveals to us that "[*Christ*] *also hath once suffered for sins, the just for the unjust, that he might bring us to God, being put to death in the flesh, but quickened by the Spirit.*" Therefore, you should tell your nonbelieving hearer that God introduced Himself, Jesus, to us so that we could be saved. We need to show the lost how God brought Jesus to this earth to make a bridge for us to get to God so that we will not have to be separated from God any longer. Jesus paid all the penalty of our guilt on the cross. God poured all of His anger, wrath, and judgment upon Jesus. The payment God demanded for our sins was the blood of His own dear Son. Hebrews 9:22 says, *"And almost all things are by the law purged with blood; and without shedding of blood is no remission."* Ephesians 1:7 declares, *"In whom we have redemption through his blood, the forgiveness of sins, according to the riches of his grace."* Hebrews 9:14 rhetorically ask the question, *"How much more shall the blood of Christ, who through the eternal Spirit offered himself without spot to God, purge your conscience from dead works to serve the living God?"* The answer to that question is that it should have been you and I on that cross bearing the punishment for our sins, but perfect Jesus did it for us. He became sin and took our punishment and paid the price for our sins. Jesus' substitutionary sacrifice on the cross is the remedy and the payment that God will accept as a substitute for our guilt and debt of sins. JESUS PAID THE PRICE!

— 6th Point —
A Person Must Believe That
Jesus Resurrected From the Dead

I want to make something clear to you. I have noticed something very sad in Christianity today amongst many Bible believing Christians. Many times, many Christians make the dire mistake to present much of the Gospel of Jesus Christ to a nonbeliever, but fail to present the victorious part of the Gospel. The part that I hear many leave out is the glorious, victorious truth that Jesus Christ physically resurrected from the dead! Without His resurrection, our faith would be in vain (1 Corinthians 15:12-19). We Christians would be people most miserable, and we would be without hope.

The Bible contains a plethora of verses referring to the bodily resurrection of Jesus Christ. For example, the Bible declares that Jesus

Christ *"was delivered for our offences, and was raised again for our justification"* in Romans 4:25. If Jesus would have just died and been buried, and that's all, then we could never really know if His sacrificial death for our sins was indeed sufficient. We would be a people with no hope. If Christ would have remained in the tomb, He would have been just another good man that lived on this earth, inspired many people for a unique cause, and then died like all the rest. But the Bible triumphantly proclaims in Acts 2:23-24 that *"Him* [Jesus], *being delivered by the determinate counsel and foreknowledge of God* [has been] *crucified and slain: Whom God hath raised up, having loosed the pains of death: because it was not possible that he should be holden of it."* Nonetheless, Jesus has indeed risen from the dead. He is the Conqueror of not only sin, but also of death! His bodily resurrection substantiates all of His claims. We can know for certain that God has accepted His blood offering for our sins, and that He is the way, He is the truth, and He is the life, as He proclaimed in John 14:6. His resurrection gives us confidence to put all our trust and hope in Him and to believe that He is the way unto God the Father and eternal life. He is not a way to God, but He is the way. Because of His resurrection, we can stand justified before our Creator. Romans 5:1 affirms, *"Therefore being justified by faith, we have peace with God through our Lord Jesus Christ."* Romans 5:9-10 confirms that *"Much more then, being now justified by his blood, we shall be saved from wrath through him. For if, when we were enemies, we were reconciled to God by the death of his Son, much more, being reconciled, we shall be saved by his life."* Finally, Titus 3:7 promises, *"That being justified by his grace, we should be made heirs according to the hope of eternal life."*

So, please do not make the dire mistake and forget to proclaim to your lost friend that Jesus Christ indeed physically arose from the dead. Romans 10:17 says, *"So then faith cometh by hearing, and hearing by the word of God,"* and Romans 10:14 asks some good questions: *"How then shall they* [the lost] *call on* [Jesus] *in whom they have not believed? and how shall they believe in him of whom they have not heard? and how shall they hear without a preacher?"* Someone cannot be saved without realizing and believing this fascinating wonderful truth that Jesus did rise from the grave. If someone does not hear this truth, they will not be able to know it, and if they do not know it, they will not be able to believe it. And, if you do not know that Jesus has the power over death, then you will not be able to have the faith to believe that He can even save you. For, He has the power over death and sin.

— 7th Point —
A Person Must Realize That
Eternal Life Is a Gift from God

Romans 6:23 states that *"For the wages of sin is death; but the gift of God is eternal life through Jesus Christ our Lord."* Eternal life cannot be earned nor is it deserved. It is only by God's grace! Eternal life is a gift that God wants to give people. A gift is a present. A gift is anything which is voluntarily transferred or bestowed by one person to another without a desire of anything in return. To put it in common language, a gift has no strings attached. You cannot do anything for a gift, or else it would not be a gift. It would be some sort of wage or an earning.

A gift is merely when one individual thinks about another and out of the kindness of his heart he gives a gift to someone else without any thought of return. If the giver of the gift would desire or solicit anything for return of any type of work, then it would not be a gift, it would be a wage. But then, think about this: All gifts come with a price. Though the receiver does not have to pay or do anything for a gift, that does not mean the gift does not have a price to be paid for it. The giver of the gift certainly had to work and earn the money to afford the gift. Then he had to go to the store, pick the gift out, pay for the gift with his hard-earned money, maybe wrap it up, and then take it to the receiver for the receiver to accept the gift. All of these things are done prior to the giver giving the gift. All of these things add up to be the price of the gift. Whether or not the receiver knows all of this is irrelevant to receiving the gift. The receiver of the gift simply has to reach out and accept or take the gift when the giver offers him the gift. Though a great price has been paid for the gift, the receiver easily accepts the gift and enjoys all the benefits of it.

The same ideal has played out with God's gift of eternal life. Though Jesus graciously went through all the extreme trouble by the shedding of His blood to pay the price for the gift of eternal life; the receiver of eternal life too cannot do anything for the gift of eternal life. He simply must believe and receive this wonderful gift that God has purchased and wants to give him.

We must help nonbelievers to see that God has eternal life and He wants to give them that gift. Not because they deserve it but because out of the kindness of His heart—He thought about them and wants to give it to them. Remember, we cannot do anything to get the gift of eternal life, nor can we do anything to keep it after we receive it. We must get a lost sinner to understand that he cannot do one little thing for salvation. We must help them to understand that God thought about them and went through all the trouble to make it possible for them to have eternal life with Him. God made it simpler than an act or a work. Ephesians 2:8-9 informs us that "*For by grace are ye saved through faith; and that not of yourselves: it is the gift of God: Not of works, lest any man should boast.*" Titus 3:5 states, "*Not by works of righteousness which we have done, but according to his mercy he saved us, by the washing of regeneration, and renewing of the Holy Ghost.*" Romans 4:5 says, "*But to him that worketh not, but believeth on him that justifieth the ungodly, his faith is counted for righteousness.*" Even the smallest percentage of works debases saving grace, as Romans 11:6 makes so pointedly clear: "*And if by grace, then is it no more of works: otherwise grace is no more grace. But if it be of works, then is it no more grace.*"

An excellent question was asked in Acts 16:30-31, "*...Sirs, what must I do to be saved?*" The excellent answer was responded, "*And they said, Believe on the Lord Jesus Christ, and thou shalt be saved, and thy house.*" This is why, in order to receive God's gift of eternal life, we must call upon the Lord Jesus to save us. We need to explain to a lost sinner that we all must believe on Jesus Christ and His work on the cross of Calvary in order to be saved. For Romans 10:13 tells us that "*For whosoever shall call upon the name of the Lord shall be saved.*" This is a promise from God.

Close the Deal

After you tell your hearer each of these truths, review the truths with him and find out whether or not he sees his need of the Savior. So many Christians who actually are going out and telling the Gospel do a good job in explaining all the points of the Gospel but then they make the big mistake not to close the deal. They have explained the Gospel thoroughly, God has revealed the Gospel to the lost sinner, and yet many Christians make the serious mistake to not bring the lost person to the feet of Jesus. They tell the Gospel to the lost soul and then afterwards they just smile and say something like—"now wasn't that good?" And then just smile and change the conversation. Now think about that or something indifferent to that effect. What a horrible shame! Here the Christian has spent ten, thirty minutes, or perhaps a few hours of each other's time going through each Gospel point. The lost sinner realizes he is lost. The lost sinner knows and desires for his sins to be washed away, but he is just left there empty-handed and not given the remedy that he so thirsts for. I beg you to please not make this grave mistake. If you have the blessed opportunity to thoroughly explain each point of the Gospel, praise God! If they understand their need and believe all the points then they are ready to come meet the Savior and begin a wonderful long-life relationship with Him. So, please close the deal. Bring them to the feet of Jesus. Do not leave them empty-handed, wondering what they should do with the Gospel.

After you review this truth with them, continue on with the wonderful last step. Romans 10:9 says, *"That if thou shalt confess with thy mouth the Lord Jesus, and shalt believe in thine heart that God hath raised him from the dead, thou shalt be saved."* John 3:18 reveals to us that *"He that believeth on him* [Jesus] *is not condemned: but he that believeth not is condemned already, because he hath not believed in the name of the only begotten Son of God."* This passage of scripture is letting us know how we can appease God's anger towards sin. God has already judged sin on the cross of Jesus Christ. For those who do not believe on Jesus Christ they will have to face God in their sin state and He will righteously judge them according to their guilt of breaking His Law. However, we should tell the lost sinner that he can be forgiven. Tell the lost sinner that this verse in the Bible is one of many verses where God is giving us His faithful promise that He is willing to save anyone who just believes with their heart on the Lord Jesus Christ. This promise of salvation comes with a stipulation, though. In order to receive the gift of salvation, an individual must believe within His heart that Jesus really did physically die and physically arose from the dead for his sins. John 3:36 affirms this promise, *"He that believeth on the Son hath everlasting life: and he that believeth not the Son shall not see life; but the wrath of God abideth on him."* Therefore inform them that they must believe that Jesus is God and that He died on the cross for their sins and that He arose from the grave for their sins.

Romans 10:13 then goes on to affirm the wonderful promise that *"For whosoever shall call upon the name of the Lord shall be saved."* After you have discussed all these truths with them, ask this question, "If we were to bow our heads right now and I were to lead us in a prayer, and since Jesus is willing to accept you just as you are, would you be willing to accept His gift of eternal life, right here right now?" If they answer, "Yes," you may perhaps want to lead them in a prayer asking for eternal life. They must mean it from their heart, but most importantly, you need to be sensitive to the Holy Spirit in leading them in a prayer. Remember, it is not the prayer that saves an individual. It is belief on the Lord Jesus Christ that saves them. A prayer is meant to be a true expression of an attitude of the heart. It is nothing more than the wonderful manifestation that God uses as a confirmation within oneself for what has already taken place within an individual's heart. You may have just taken a person through a phenomenal presentation of the Gospel, and he may have said some words about Christ coming into his heart, but if the words did not come from his heart, that's all they were: words.

For this reason, never; and I repeat, never tell an individual that he is saved! We are not God. We cannot see their soul. We can only hope that they truly believe on Jesus, but we can never be for certain, as we are not God. All we can do is exhort people around us with the Word and allow God to do His work. Our duty is to speak the Word. God's work is to convict, convince, and convert a soul. The Holy Spirit's work according to Romans 8:16 is to enlighten someone to know that they are a child of God. The people's work is to believe and receive His gift.

For those who profess Jesus as their Savior in front of me, as an example, I personally like to use the following and say something to this effect to them: "Praise God...Now for those who truly believe on Jesus for their salvation, Jesus promises that He indeed saves that person. God is faithful to His promises. He does not lie. Now I want to encourage you by showing you one of Jesus' many promises ..." This way they can be encouraged through God's own Word and at the same time I may or may not be making a tragic mistake of acting as God and declaring someone is saved or not.

Then I do go into more scriptures with them. Many times I take them to the book of 1 John in the back of the Bible because this little book contains a lot of truth regarding salvation and informs us of many promises to those individuals who trust on Jesus. One passage of scripture that I have many times taken a new believer is to 1 John 5:11-13. The passage says, *"And this is the record, that God hath given to us eternal life, and this life is in his Son. He that hath the Son hath life; and he that hath not the Son of God hath not life. These things have I written unto you that believe on the name of the Son of God; that ye may know that ye have eternal life, and that ye may believe on the name of the Son of God."* Another verse is 1 John 2:25, which states, *"And this is the promise that he hath promised us, even eternal life."* However, if I want to use some other similar promises from other books of the Bible, a good passage of scripture I have taken new believers is to John 10:28-29 which states, *"And I give unto them eternal life; and they shall never perish, neither shall any man pluck them out of my hand. My Father, which gave them me, is greater than all; and no man is able to pluck them out of my Father's hand."* There certainly are many other verses that I sometimes use too. Some of those other verses which are expedient and useful are Philippians 1:6, Romans 8:1, 1 Peter 1:5, John 5:24, John 6:37, and countless others. More importantly, I simply find it best to depend on the Holy Spirit to guide me in to which verses they need to hear and not what I think they need to hear.

An Important Warning

To sum it all up, a wholly felt belief in the Gospel of Jesus Christ is the only way to have our sins washed away and to go to Heaven. Some good questions to consider and bring up in order to present an opportunity to tell the Gospel message to people are: Are you sure you will go to Heaven? If you were to die today, do you know for sure that you would go to Heaven, or do you have some doubt? If you are in doubt today, you can know for sure. If you know someone else who is not saved, you can tell him how he can know for sure that Heaven is his eternal home!

Bear in remembrance an admonition from God to us in Galatians 1:8-9: "*But though we, or an angel from heaven, preach any other gospel unto you than that which we have preached unto you, let him be accursed. As we said before, so say I now again, if any man preach any other gospel unto you than that ye have received, let him be accursed.*" Therefore, I encourage you to study and thoroughly know the Gospel of Jesus Christ. Jesus proclaimed in John 14:6: "*I am the way, THE TRUTH, and the life: no man cometh unto the Father, but by me* [emphasis added]." The Bible clearly teaches us that we must seek truth because the natural mind is not subject to the law of God. The scripture tells us we must rightly divide the Word of truth (2 Timothy 2:15). Also, 2 John 1:9-10 says, "[*H*]*e that abideth in the doctrine of Christ, he hath both the Father and the Son. If there come any unto you, and bring not this doctrine, receive him not into your house, neither bid him God speed.*"

Again, I encourage you to study and thoroughly know the simple Gospel message of Jesus Christ. The Gospel of Christ is simple (2 Corinthians 11:3) and it is straightforward truth (John 17:17). If anyone preaches a different gospel, other than the simple Gospel of Jesus Christ, the Bible warns that such an individual is to be accursed. That means to be damned, detestable, abominable, and doomed. While you are learning the simplicity of the Gospel and learning to be able to prove it through different scriptures of the Bible, keep in mind to avoid any ungodly doctrines, which at their surface might deceitfully appear right, but underneath they maliciously distort the cross of Jesus Christ and His Gospel. Some examples of distorted evil doctrines are: You must work to earn and/or to keep eternal life, reliance upon baptism to be saved, the abominable doctrine that God will take away your salvation if you do not work enough for Him, and the devilish doctrine that it is okay to pray to Jesus along with any other "good" person who knew Him. This particular demonic inspired distortion includes believing in or praying to "saints" or dead men like Joseph Smith. Other distorted doctrines which we are to avoid are: That you must speak in tongues to receive the Holy Spirit, Jesus Christ was not raised from the grave on the third day, or you must follow some type of sacraments in order to earn God's grace. All of these and every single other type of distorted doctrines, and the like, are straight from the pit of Hell and are cause for any such proclaimer of these doctrines to be accursed. These are not Bible doctrines. They are not found in God's Word, the Holy Bible. They are deceitful damnable doctrines of demons and such men are to be avoided and to be accursed (1 Timothy 4:1 and Hebrews 13:9).

Alternatively, I encourage you to stay focused on Jesus Christ and Jesus Christ alone! Practice showing people some of the verses that proclaim each point of the Gospel of Jesus Christ. Practice listening and obeying the Holy Spirit's leadings. His voice always points us closer to Jesus and nothing else. His voice always points us to the Bible which points us closer to Jesus (John 15:26). By doing all of that, you may be able to accomplish what 1 Corinthians 9:18 asserts, "[*Verily*] *that, when I preach the gospel, I may make the gospel of Christ without charge, that I abuse not my power in the gospel*." And before you know it, you will be on a joyful, exciting, and rewarding road of great investments in the lives of people.

CHAPTER 4

Two Ways You Witness

Even so hath the Lord ordained that they which
preach the gospel should live of the gospel.
– 1 Corinthians 9:14

I do not know who first said it, but there is an old saying that is very true: "Your walk talks and your talk talks, but your walk talks louder than your talk talks." Whether you talk for Jesus or not, you certainly are influencing people by how you "walk," or live. People are always watching and observing you. In the context of Hebrews 12:1, we are reminded that we are always being watched. I am aware of the discussion within Christendom relating to whom these people might be referring to in this verse. But more importantly, I look at the application, and the point of the application is that we indeed are being watched. We might not know when or by whom, but we are being carefully watched (see also 1 Corinthians 4:9, Daniel 4:17 and 1 Timothy 6:12). One of the important points of this verse is that people are always observing us and keeping and paying attention to the words we speak and the lifestyles we live. This can be a good thing or a bad thing. With people observing us all the time, the reality is that we influence people in two ways, the same two ways we can witness for Jesus: speaking with our lips to people and speaking through our lifestyle before them. It's that simple! The two work hand-in-hand and are essentially two sides of the same coin.

Do you remember Acts 1:8? It reads, *"But ye shall receive power, after that the Holy Ghost is come upon you: and ye shall be witnesses unto me both in Jerusalem, and in all Judea, and in Samaria, and unto the uttermost part of the earth."* Yes, this verse was speaking about those certain individuals in the passage who were to wait for God to empower them. Nonetheless, its application is so relevant for us Christians today, too. Today, this verse applies to us in that it is more of an expectation of something that we would certainly be willing to do, knowing that even if God had not commanded us, we would still do it. God said, "*and ye shall be witnesses*" to people near you, such as within your local community, and out to people all around the world. It is good to know that God is a God who empowers His people to witness on His behalf. It is good to know that we can be a witness for Him through two ways: our mouths and through a holy lifestyle. However, before we look at these two ways to see how we can use them to witness to people in a practical sense, it is a good idea to review what Jesus has commanded us to do. Thankfully, Jesus knew some of us would overlook that authoritative expectation mentioned in Acts 1:8, so as a reminder, He commissioned us in Matthew 28:19-20 to "*Go ye therefore, and teach all nations…Teaching them to observe all things whatsoever I have commanded you.*" This means we are to go out and use our lives and our mouths to witness to people. Jesus commanded another time in Mark 16:15, saying, "*Go ye into all the world, and preach the Gospel to every creature.*" At another time, Jesus, in Matthew 10:7, instructed us to preach to people that the Kingdom of Heaven is at hand. The word "preach" means to proclaim or to give earnest advice. And guess what? The only way we can proclaim or to give earnest advice to people is for us to use our mouths to do so.

The command is given to all Christians. Not just to pastors, but to all followers of Jesus. God commissions all Christians to go out and witness on His behalf, no matter our age, personality, outlook on life, or what our talents may or may not be. Since God gave this commission to all Christians, He also has given us examples in the Bible of His commissioning people of different ages, personalities, outlooks on life, and talents. That is because God knows the commission is for all Christians, not just a small group of individuals with certain attributes.

God wants to use people of all attributes and characteristics. For example, we can look at four distinguished men in the Bible as examples: Isaiah, Jeremiah, Ezekiel, and Moses. Each man was entirely different and each was of a totally different age group when they realized they were to publish God's Word with their mouths. Jeremiah was a boy (Jeremiah 1:7); Isaiah was a young man, (Isaiah 6:5); Ezekiel was around 30 years old (Ezekiel 1:3); and Moses was an older man (Acts 7:23, 30-34). However, God commissioned them all and called them to go speak His Word. Even their personalities and outlooks on life were very different, but each man was commissioned the same: to go speak on God's behalf. For example, Isaiah and Jeremiah were extreme opposites. Isaiah was loud, impetuous, optimistic, and full of enthusiasm. However, Jeremiah was quiet and pessimistic, and he felt unworthy to do God's work.

Again, God wants to use the lives of children, teenagers, men, and women in their productive years of life, and certainly even the elderly people who have accumulated the wisdom and knowledge of many years. God commissions all Christians in every type of life. He wants all people to go out and proclaim His Gospel. God is abundantly rich to teach us knowledge and give us wisdom regarding how to be a proficient, effective soulwinner. God is even gracious enough to allow people to re-enlist to do His work who had previously quit and sat on the sidelines of life. God wants to use all ages and all personalities of people. All we have to do is make ourselves available to Him and obey His commission: to go out and witness.

Using Our Mouths

Now, here's some good news. God never tells us to do something He has not demonstrated Himself. As we look at the first way we can witness, we shall be exhorted to use our mouths, even as God Himself has used the instrument of the mouth to speak His own Word.

God allows us to know that even He uses His mouth to speak, and that is to speak things into life, being, and for significance. In Isaiah 55:11, God says, "*So shall my word be that goeth forth out of my mouth: it shall not return unto me void, but it shall accomplish that which I please, and it shall prosper in the thing whereto I sent it.*" God's Word is matchless. It was by His spoken Word that God created everything. God used his mouth and said, "*Let there be light.*" And there was light (Genesis 1:3). When Jesus was on the earth, He demonstrated this simple action of using one's mouth, too. He taught with words coming out of His mouth and lips, and when He spoke, His words had a powerful, lasting effect on people. His words angered some and broke the hearts of others. His words softened the hearts of some and hardened the hearts of others. When Jesus spoke, things happened. Jesus healed people by speaking. Jesus forgave sins by speaking. He always used his mouth. For example, in Luke 5:20, Jesus used his mouth and awesomely declared, "*Man, thy sins are forgiven thee.*" In John 11:43, He raised the dead by speaking. Crying out with a loud voice, He commanded, "*Lazarus, come forth.*" Jesus spoke softly and calmed the wind and sea with His soft rebuke, "*Peace, be still,*" in Mark 4:39. In Matthew 8:32, He cast out demons by one word from His lips: "*Go.*"

Jesus could have just mentally thought actions into existence. He could have performed miracles with only the thinking of His mind, and the miracles still would have occurred and brought change. Jesus did not have to use his lips and mouth to bring about change in the lives of many people. Nonetheless, Jesus chose to use His mouth as an example for us, so that as we notice that God uses His mouth, tongue, and lips to express His Word, then we little humans definitely need to do the same. God gave us a mouth, lips, and a tongue. We should be good stewards of them and use them for His glory—A glory that stimulates change and life in the lives of people through the power of His Word.

As we use our mouths to witness to others, we need to remember God has entrusted us with the Gospel. Therefore, I like how the man

Balaam, in Numbers 23:12, put it, *"must* [we] *not take heed to speak that which the LORD hath put in* [our] *mouths?* God is permitting you and I to represent Him and His Kingdom and His Word. We are allowed by God to be mouthpieces for Him (Malachi 2:7). First Thessalonians 2:4 reminds us that even as we speak, we are to speak on His behalf to others, with this important caution: *"not as pleasing men, but God."* Each time we speak, we should be motivated by this truth to speak only to please God, and no one else. We do not speak for the approval of any man. The approval of men does not matter one bit. We are to do and speak for what God approves of. If we do that, then the work of soulwinning becomes easier as we realize that the fear of men is insignificant. The Apostle Paul realized this, and therefore he was able to write in Galatians 1:10, *"For do I now persuade men, or God? or do I seek to please men? for if I yet pleased men, I should not be the servant of Christ."* How wonderful is that? Each time you and I use our mouths to speak the Gospel, we are reminded that we are using our mouthpieces to please Christ.

Yes, it is true. If we are going to use our mouths and speak on God's behalf to please Him, then many times the message of the Gospel that we speak to people will most generally not be what they want to hear. Though this be true, we still need to speak the message they need to hear, not the message they want to hear. The Gospel always will destroy man's pride. The Gospel never paints an attractive picture of man's depraved, sinful heart. However, for those few who do recognize that they are totally worthy of Hell and are in great need of the Savior, then the Gospel will be pleasing words to their ears, and they will be eager to listen and hear the good news that God has for them, through the utterance of our lips. And, in speaking the Gospel to people, we should never use flattery to try to win them over to the Kingdom of God. If we use flattery, then we would be lying to another individual and giving them a false pride, because flattery involves saying to a person's face what you would never say behind his or her back. Flattery is excessive or insincere admiration. There is nothing admirable about mankind except that we are rotten sinners who need the Savior. One such example found in the Bible, in which we can learn why we should not use flattery, is through the life of the Apostle Paul. In writing to the Christians in Thessalonica, he used his testimony to implicitly admonish them from using flattery (1 Thessalonians 2:5). He understood the vile self-centeredness that births flattery from a person's heart and out of a person's mouth. Therefore, he warned against it. In addition, this admonishment against flattery in the scriptures was not restricted only to the writings of the Apostle Paul. God warns us repeatedly in the scriptures to avoid speaking flattery. Proverbs 29:5, Proverbs 26:28, and Psalm 12:3-4 are texts that describe the destructions brought about from the unwholesome motives of flatterers. Flattery absolutely can never attract sinners to the Gospel of our Lord Jesus Christ, who, by the way, did the opposite of flattery by completely emptying Himself and giving up all for sinners. Consequently, we had better steer away from using flattery and be humbly honest with people we come into contact with.

Two Tools Our Mouths Can Use to Compel the Gospel to Someone

As we go out into the world and speak to people around us to compel them to repent and put their trust in Jesus, there are two tools we can use in order to speak the power of the Gospel to them. Those two tools that God has given each Christian are our personal testimony and the Word of God.

The Tool of Our Testimony

First, each Christian has a testimony. Our testimony is our individual life story of what God has done in our own lives. Each one of us has a powerful testimony. No Christian's testimony is useless; instead, each Christian has a testimony that is a powerful, effectual, and valuable resource. Revelation 12:11 confirms that each one of us has a powerful testimony that is useful in this spiritual war around us. This scripture teaches us that our personal story is so powerful that it is one of the weapons God has given us to overcome Satan, the devil himself. If the word of our testimony is that powerful, in regards that our testimony can and will eventually assist in overcoming the prince of this world, Satan, than how much more powerful is it to overcome another human's disbelief and to persuade him or her to be saved? You already know the answer—it is that powerful! Do not think otherwise. Your spoken testimony is powerful. Satan knows it, and this is why Christians are always hearing those thoughts in our minds to keep silent and not to tell others our personal testimony of what Christ has done for us. Satan understands that when a Christian speaks his testimony to other individuals, he (Satan) is just that much closer to losing the battle in someone's life (Revelation 12:11).

Each Christian's testimony has three parts to it, according to Acts 26:4-23. Your personal testimony is your story of: (1) Who you were before you knew Jesus as your Savior, (2) How you came to meet and know Jesus as your Savior, and (3) What Jesus has been doing in your life since you came to know Him. Here is the best thing about your testimony: You alone are the best person to tell your story! You are the authority on your life. You lived it. You are the one who has been experiencing it. No one else has been there every single second, as you have. As a result, you know it best. You can recall it best. You can understand and feel the pains, the triumphs, the concerns, and the glorious times of it all. You and I should testify to people around us about the miraculous work that Jesus has done and has been continuing to do in our lives. First Chronicles 16:8 and Psalm 105:1 both instruct us to "*Make known His deeds among the peoples!*" Hence, we are commanded to go out and tell people about Christ's mighty deeds that He has done for us, such as how he saved us. Accordingly, I exhort you to go out, use your mouth, and tell your personal testimony to people. As you speak your testimony more and more to people, you will notice He will bring people into your life who will best relate to it, and then you will notice Jesus bringing about the fruit of souls that results from telling the good news of Himself.

The Tool of the Holy Bible

Our testimony is a powerful tool that God has given us to speak to people. Nonetheless, the other tool we can use with our mouths to tell people the Gospel is the Bible itself. We should tell people what the Bible actually says. Most people in general do not read the Bible; they have very limited knowledge of what it says about judgment, salvation, Hell, Heaven, God, and Jesus. We do not need to have a thorough and profound knowledge of God's Word to speak the truths of the Bible to people. If all we know is that we are sinners who need Jesus and we have to believe on His death and resurrection for salvation, then that is sufficient to tell people and actually win their souls to Christ. If you recall, it was all that the Samaritan woman had in John chapter 4, and many believed because of the simple and uncomplicated Word they heard from her lips.

Now, I strongly do encourage you to study, memorize, meditate, and become very familiar with verses in your Bible. It is very helpful if we know at least some scriptures from the Bible. For example, we can talk to people and lovingly warn them that the Bible informs us that God gave us His Law—The Ten Commandments—to live by. Then we can tell them that we have broken His Law, such as the ninth commandment: *"Thou shalt not bear false witness."* Then after showing this law to people we can show how we are guilty and on our way to Hell. Then we can talk to them about how much God really does love us; that He does not desire for us to die and be judged and go to Hell. Finally, we can talk to them about what the Bible says about salvation; that we need to believe that Jesus died on the cross for our sins and that He arose from the grave for our sins—that we can put our trust in Jesus and that God will forgive us of our sins and put our sins on Jesus.

When we speak to another person about the Gospel, then God, through the words we speak, is either giving them faith or building up their faith so that they can be able to eventually place their trust and life into the hands of Jesus Christ. The Bible says in Romans 10:17 that *"faith cometh by hearing, and hearing by the word of God."*

Using Our Lifestyles

I have said a lot about our mouths and how they can be used as a witness for Jesus. Just as our mouth can and should be used as a microphone for Christ's Gospel, our lifestyle can and should be a mirror of Christ's Gospel to those around us. Our lifestyle is just as important as, if not more important than, what comes out of our mouths. For 1 John 3:18 says, *"My little children, let us not love in word, neither in tongue; but in deed and in truth."* Our walk talks and our talk talks, but our walk talks louder than our talk talks. The credibility of what we say is through our testimony in our lifestyle. Whether or not we talk for Jesus, we certainly are influencing people by how we live. People are always watching us. Our lips do the talking, but our actions and our lifestyle do the walking in life. Not only do we witness with our lips, but we also witness through our actions and lifestyle. For this I say: may our living testimony influence people toward wanting to hear the message of the Gospel from our lips.

Nevertheless, this is not always the case. The Apostle Paul, in Galatians chapter 2, noticed that Peter and some other Christians were not living uprightly according to the truth of the Gospel message. In Galatians 2:14 he questioned their actions and further rebuked them for their hypocritical actions that did not match their Gospel message. Shamefully, today, some Christians still work only with their mouths. They profess the Gospel, but their actions speak contrary to the Gospel. This should not be so. For the Lord, in 1 Corinthians 9:14, instructs us against such hypocrisy, saying, *"Even so hath the Lord ordained that they which preach the gospel should live of the gospel."* God wants more than just our mouths. He wants that part of us that is on the ground too: our entire bodies! The Christians who give not only their mouths for God's use, but also their bodies will quickly discover that God will mercifully work to persuade them to let go of a lot of things they have held onto with a death-like grip. If Christians do not let go of those things they hold onto so tightly, then their grip, holding onto the wrong things, will disable their ability to reach out to people and be useful to win their souls to Christ.

An important principle that James 1:14-15 teaches us is that our lifestyle stems from habits that stem from simple daily chosen actions. Our actions are revealed through our physical bodies. And our physical bodies consist of the head as well as the hands and feet and all of the bodily essentials. God wants our brains, as well as our bones and muscles. God wants every fiber of our being to be used for His testimony. In thinking about this awesome truth, it should convince us that we ought to do our best thinking for the Lord. We ought to eat the best food for God. We ought to mobilize our body in the holiest and safest actions possible for God, and we ought to work our best for Him. Not only to have our godly actions to be a witness to people, but to have our godly actions in order to please God. Then, He shall be glorified. If there is a more holy motivation to live a life that speaks His Gospel to people than that, then I would like to know it.

When we live a life that pleases and glorifies God, people do notice it. Our outward holy lifestyle then lures people into our surroundings to hear the Gospel message from our mouths. If we choose actions in our lives that do not glorify God, then people will either question the message of the Gospel from our lips or they will totally reject it. This is why unholy actions and lifestyles offer nonbelievers an implausible reason to reject the Gospel. Ungodly lifestyles present nonbelievers with reasons of why not to come to the God who these Christians claim can change a heart and life of an individual. Before nonbelievers will believe the Gospel from our lips, they want to see the evidence from our lifestyles that the Gospel actually does work.

John 12:46 shows us that Jesus came into the world as the Light for the world. Then Matthew 5:14 teaches us that we Christians are a light to the world. So, we learn that Christ is the inherent Light. He abides inside those who place their trust in Him. Though we Christians are not the Light that saves, we are the lights of the world that can and should reflect Christ (the Principal Light). We only can reflect Christ by the lifestyle we choose. Our lifestyle can and should reflect who and what He is. Matthew 5:16 instructs us to *"let* [our] *light so shine before men, that they may see* [our] *good works, and glorify* [our] *Father which is in Heaven."* Again, followers of Jesus do not have inherent light; rather we have reflective light. Jesus is the inherent Light. As we live a life that is pleasing and honorable before God, we then reflect His light to the world.

Therefore, we need to make sure that nothing comes between us and the Lord's light, or our light will not shine as brightly for others to see. For example, God has instructed in 2 Corinthians 6:17 for us to come out of the world and to be separate or different. To come out from among the ungodly and to be separate does not mean for us to leave our daily responsibilities and go live afar off in the middle of a forest separate from civilization. It means to be distinctive in our character, mannerisms, and speech. We cannot save ungodly men if we remain participant among them in the same sinful elements with them. A sinner will not convert another sinner. An ungodly individual will not convert another ungodly individual. A dark-minded individual will not convert an individual of darkness. Thus, a worldly Christian will not convert individuals of the world.

The only way we will be able to shine in the midst of a confusing and conflicting world is to be different in a holy manner, by imitating Jesus Christ. Hebrews 13:8 informs us that Jesus is the same yesterday, today and forever. Therefore, His morals, conducts, standards and ways of life are the same today as they were years ago, and they will be the same tomorrow as they were in times past. Cultural trends, fads, and customs come and go and change all the time in relation to the people of a particular generation and location on the earth. Even the world's morals change; some decades they become cleaner, and other decades they become dirtier. The world's standards of life waver up and down and are unstable in what is supposedly the norm. We Christians are not to be influenced into our cultural trends, fads, and ways of life. We are called to come out and be different! We are to be godly. Godly means "God's way"—not the world's way, but God's way! If we are living by the world's way, then we are ungodly. If we are ungodly, then His light definitely is not going to reflect from our lives as a testimony for the Gospel of Jesus Christ. This is why Christians should be diligent to seek God's Word and find out how we are to talk, dress, and act. We should seek to find out what music God only ascribes for us to listen to and sing for His glory and not for the glory or comfort of our emotions. Really, we owe God the due respect and diligence to seek Him and find out what He wants (2 Chronicles 7:14). We also should find out what God is pleased with and what He is not pleased with. The things He is pleased with and the things that bring honor to Him, we should do in order to reflect Christ; the things God is not for we should disregard from inclusion of our lives. If we do this, then we might be able to "*walk worthy of the Lord unto all pleasing, being fruitful in every good work, and increasing in the knowledge of God,*" as Colossians 1:10 exhorts us to do. For 1 John 2:6 gives us the heed that "*He that saith he abideth in him* [Jesus] *ought himself also so to walk, even as he walked.*"

How to Speak and Live the Gospel

God wants the inherent Light, Jesus, to shine out of us Christians and unto the darkened world. Since this is His desire, He has provided us with a colossal amount of scripture texts for our instruction and understanding in how we are to live. The volumes of scriptures in regards to an outward holy life are provided to us so that we might know how God wants to shine Himself through us before this filthy, unstable world. While the Bible does indicate that men should be able to see Christ shining through our good works in order to glorify our Father which is in Heaven (Matthew 5:16), it is not these works that result in the salvation of lost souls. Remember, Romans 1:16 informs us that the Gospel itself is the power of God unto salvation. First Corinthians 1:21 tells us that, "*it pleased God by the foolishness of preaching to save them that believe.*" It does not say, it pleased God by the foolishness of living a holy lifestyle to save them that believe. Subsequently, it is wise to live the life of Christ in front of people so that they can listen without being distracted by an ungodly lifestyle. Therefore, I exhort you to live a godly life and be wise with your mouth to present the Gospel with your lips so that the power of salvation, the Gospel, can be heard and released into the hearts of the lost. Then their hearts can be convicted of sin and converted to the Lord Jesus Christ.

Here is a list of just some of the volume of verses that God has given us in instruction of how we are to conduct ourselves in speech and action. I encourage you not to overlook these verses but to actually read them, then meditate on them and seek the Lord to help you to apply them into your life. I would also encourage you to get into your Bible and do a study on how you are to conduct yourself and how you are to communicate amongst people. May these scriptures be a blessing of conviction in your heart and a resource to draw you closer to the Savior.

I would like to start off with the verse that pivots all other verses and compiles them all into one single simple instruction; that is 1 Thessalonians 5:22: *"Abstain from all appearance of evil."* That simple! God certainly knows how to wrap up all godly ways into one simple statement: *"ABSTAIN FROM ALL APPEARANCE OF EVIL* [emphasis added]." If you might be wondering what the "evil" may be referring to, I'll tell you. Evil refers to anything ungodly, self-centered, prideful, or wicked. The word "abstain" means that a person is to hold oneself back voluntarily from doing something. Therefore, this verse means that if something has just a slight sense of ungodliness, we are to abstain and get away from it; either choice of action or conduct. If you have the slightest reservations whether something would be dishonorable to God, then wisdom would tell you to abstain from it. Now, we do live in a sinful world, so I am not stating that we go live in a monastery and abstain from the world. Jesus in John 17:15-17 prayed against such segregated actions. He prayed to God the Father: *"I pray not that thou shouldest take them out of the world, but that thou shouldest keep them from the evil. They are not of the world, even as I am not of the world. Sanctify them through thy truth: thy word is truth."* Consequently, we learn that we indeed are to live in this world amongst the nonbelievers, but we should be distinct by living with an attitude and heart that seeks to please God and to know His truth for choices in righteous living.

As I mentioned earlier, here are some of the many encouraging scriptures that instruct us how we are to righteously live in this sinful world:

Philippians 1:27 states, *"Only let your conversation* [our speech as well as our conduct] *be as it becometh the gospel of Christ: that whether*

I come and see you, or else be absent, I may hear of your affairs, that ye stand fast in one spirit, with one mind striving together for the faith of the gospel." Our conduct should reveal our heavenly citizenship. We believers should gather together as much as possible so that we can encourage each other's faith and unite in one common faith of our Lord Jesus Christ.

Philippians 2:14-16 instructs us to "*Do all things without murmurings and disputings: That ye may be blameless and harmless, the sons of God, without rebuke, in the midst of a crooked and perverse nation, among whom ye shine as lights in the world; Holding forth the word of life; that I may rejoice in the day of Christ, that I have not run in vain, neither laboured in vain.*" Verse 15 of this passage focuses on the testimony of Christians. The purpose of the command in verse 14 is that the Christian might be light bearers in this world who are found to be blameless. If a Christian is to have a testimony in his community, then he has to be blameless in his actions and attitudes, both inside and outside the church. We are to be without blot or blemish, untainted by sin.

Colossians 2:6-7 shows us that "*As ye have therefore received Christ Jesus the Lord, so walk ye in him: Rooted and built up in him, and stablished in the faith, as ye have been taught, abounding therein with thanksgiving.*" Make a note that the word "rooted" denotes a complete action. We need to daily make a firm decision and carry out godly actions, which assist us to walk a life that is in Christ. Such "complete actions" will be filled with words and attitudes of thanksgiving, and grounded in faith no matter what is happening.

First Peter 2:12 warns us to be honest. It says, "*Having your conversation honest among the Gentiles: that, whereas they speak against you as evildoers, they may by your good works, which they shall behold, glorify God in the day of visitation.*" Not only are we instructed to have our conversations and conduct to be honest, but the verse also goes into detail of why we are to be honest—so that people around us will indeed take a notice of our honest lifestyles and they will eventually only be able to glorify God. How awesome is that?!

First John 2:6 reveals: *"He that saith he abideth in him [Jesus] ought himself also so to walk, even as he walked."* Abiding is habitual obedience. It has the idea of settling down in Christ or resting in Him. It is evidenced by a life modeled after Christ. This admonition to live by the teaching of Jesus reveals that this conformity starts with a decision within us (Deuteronomy 5:29). Slaves must follow the command of their masters or they will be punished. Employees must do their work to keep their jobs. Christians, who are the children of God, must obey their Father to see Him glorify Himself in and through their lives. We are to obey with a sincere desire to do so, not because God commands us to do so, but because we sincerely want to please our Father. It should be a joy to follow in the footsteps of the One who died for us.

Colossians 3:12-17 says, *"Put on therefore, as the elect of God, holy and beloved, bowels of mercies, kindness, humbleness of mind, meekness, longsuffering; Forbearing one another, and forgiving one another, if any man have a quarrel against any: even as Christ forgave you, so also do ye. And above all these things put on charity, which is the bond of perfectness. And let the peace of God rule in your hearts, to the which also ye are called in one body; and be ye thankful. Let the word of Christ dwell in you richly in all wisdom; teaching and admonishing one another in psalms and hymns and spiritual songs, singing with grace in your hearts to the Lord. And whatsoever ye do in word or deed, do all in the name of the Lord Jesus, giving thanks to God and the Father by him."* These verses are filled with so many wise instructions, it would be beneficial for you to just stop and meditate for a week or two on these verses alone, and also to apply the obedience of them into the routines of your life. They consist about how we are to interact and be with people. God lovingly shows us that we are to be kind, humble, meek, and longsuffering with people. We need to forbear with people, and not only that, but in forbearing we should have an attitude and actions to get underneath people's problems and be a real support for them. He then reminds us that we need to love people and have peace with people. Following that, He gets more personal and shows us that our hearts, our attitudes, and our mouths should abound with spiritual songs, hymns, Christ-centered music, and gracious words that just bring praise and adoration to our Savior Jesus Christ. Not the very least, but lastly, we certainly need to be thankful people. We need to go around thanking people as well as thanking God all the time for the big and little things in life. When is the last time you went around thanking God and people for _____? You fill in the blank.

I know I have presented many passages of scripture to you that explain how we are to live displaying our appreciation for God and demonstrating a true witness of Christ before the eyes and ears of the world. I would strongly suggest to you that after you finish reading this chapter that you not read any more of this book for at least a few days. Instead I suggest that you just meditate on these verses and allow God to speak profoundly to you. You will receive more help from the Lord if you take the time and meditate on these verses rather than just quickly read through this book. Although I may be sharing some good wisdom with you that the Lord has given me, all of my words are just commentary. Commentary might be tasty, but it is just baby food for your hunger. The scriptures that I have provided you are directly from the Bible. God's Word is the greater wisdom and if you meditate on His Word, you will be fed Heavenly food straight from God Himself, which is much tastier and greater than baby food.

In light of what I just said, here are some other valuable passages that you can read and mediate on too. I hope that you do mediate on these verses and that you seek God to apply these attitudes and actions into your life. Romans 12:1-2 says, *"I beseech you therefore, brethren,* by the mercies of God, that ye present your bodies a living sacrifice, holy, acceptable unto God, which is your reasonable service. And be not conformed to this world: but be ye transformed by the renewing of your mind, that ye may prove what is that good, and acceptable, and perfect, will of God."

Romans 12:9-21 instructs us that we are to "Let love be without dissimulation. Abhor that which is evil; cleave to that which is good. Be kindly affectioned one to another with brotherly love; in honour preferring one another; Not slothful in business; fervent in spirit; serving the Lord; Rejoicing in hope; patient in tribulation; continuing instant in prayer; Distributing to the necessity of saints; given to hospitality. Bless them which persecute you: bless, and curse not. Rejoice with them that do rejoice, and weep with them that weep. Be of the same mind one toward another. Mind not high things, but condescend to men of low estate. Be not wise in your own conceits. Recompense to no man evil for evil. Provide things honest in the sight of all men. If it be possible, as much as lieth in you, live peaceably with all men. Dearly beloved, avenge not yourselves, but rather give place unto wrath: for it is written, Vengeance is mine; I will repay, saith the Lord. Therefore if thine enemy hunger, feed him; if he thirst, give him drink: for in so doing thou shalt heap coals of fire on his head. Be not overcome of evil, but overcome evil with good."

Then Ephesians 4:31-32 commands us: "Let all bitterness, and wrath, and anger, and clamour, and evil speaking, be put away from you, with all malice: And be ye kind one to another, tenderhearted, forgiving one another, even as God for Christ's sake hath forgiven you."

Ephesians 5:2 tells us: "And walk in love, as Christ also hath loved us, and hath given himself for us an offering and a sacrifice to God for a sweetsmelling savour."

Keep in mind that Proverbs 11:9 admonishes that "an hypocrite with his mouth destroyeth his neighbour."

We have already looked at some verses from the book of Philippians. I have chosen many verses from this particular book because this small book is full with much instruction on good habits and lifestyles. Keep in mind that these wonderful instructions were written by Paul when he was in a cold deep dungeon. One particularly awesome section in this book is Philippians 4:4-9 which states, *"Rejoice in the Lord alway: and again I say, Rejoice. Let your moderation be known unto all men. The Lord is at hand. Be careful for nothing; but in every thing by prayer and supplication with thanksgiving let your requests be made known unto God. And the peace of God, which passeth all understanding, shall keep your hearts and minds through Christ Jesus. Finally, brethren, whatsoever things are true, whatsoever things are honest, whatsoever things are just, whatsoever things are pure, whatsoever things are lovely, whatsoever things are of good report; if there be any virtue, and if there be any praise, think on these things. Those things, which ye have both learned, and received, and heard, and seen in me, do: and the God of peace shall be with you."* If Paul was able to express these encouraging instructions for the heart to believers while he was in a cold, dark dungeon, then you and I are certainly able to possess the same attitudes in Christ Jesus.

Oh, and we cannot forget the wonderful instructions found in 1 Corinthians 10:31-33. These three verses tell us: *"Whether therefore ye eat, or drink, or whatsoever ye do, do all to the glory of God. Give none offence, neither to the Jews, nor to the Gentiles, nor to the church of God: Even as I please all men in all things, not seeking mine own profit, but the profit of many, that they may be saved."* Doing all for the glory of God involves encouraging fellow Christians and spreading the good news about Jesus Christ. Paul accomplished this by refusing to offend Jews, Greeks, or the Christians, even if it meant restricting his personal freedom. Like Christ, Paul did not seek his own will or way of life. He did not live for his own pleasure. Instead, he desired to help others. He put people before him. This should be our desire and lifestyle as well.

In another passage, Hebrews 12:1-2a, we are once more reminded: *"Wherefore seeing we also are compassed about with so great a cloud of witnesses, let us lay aside every weight, and the sin which doth so easily beset us, and let us run with patience the race that is set before us, Looking unto Jesus."* There it is! We are to look unto Jesus. If we look unto Him then all of these instructions can naturally happen in and through us by His power. It is certain that we are not capable of doing any of the numerous actions on our own (Galatians 5:17). Jesus revealed to us in Matthew 5:3 that we are poor. We are spiritually bankrupt. That is why we need to live as Galatians 2:20 says: *"I am crucified with Christ: nevertheless I live; yet not I, but Christ liveth in me: and the life which I now live in the flesh I live by the faith of the Son of God."* On the contrary, none of these instructions can happen in or through us if we are not looking unto Jesus. If we are not abiding in Him, then our carnal flesh is going to show its sinful lusts. Nonetheless, Jesus most assuredly can do every single one of these attitudes and actions through us when we look and focus on Him.

Looking at all of these truths reminds of me of the story of Philip in Acts 8:26-35. Philip obeyed the Lord's simple command to go talk to a man, an Ethiopian eunuch. Not only did he go to the eunuch, but also the passage reveals to us that he ran up to the eunuch. Philip then proceeded to use his mouth and he explained the Gospel to the man and led him to Christ for salvation. As Philip did, we are to use our lives and purposefully go up to people and use our mouths to preach unto them Jesus. The message of our lips must be matched with the message of our lives. Philip ran to the man. Running shows passion and excitement. We too must have lifestyles that are passionate for Jesus and people. We must have fervor in our going to them so we can compellingly tell them the Gospel. We must not only believe the Gospel, but we must behave the Gospel, and walk worthy of it. Those who bear the holy Gospel must have holy lives. The Gospel must not go out to people through word only, but also in power and in the Holy Ghost with much assurance through lives that glorify God. May our hearers never be able to say, "Your inconsistent life speaks so loud I cannot hear your message." Those who teach the truth must be walking in the truth (3 John 1:4). We are humans, so we will not be perfect, but let us try to live to be blameless among the lost sinners of the world (Philippians 2:15). Then they will only be able to say, "Your lifestyle speaks so loudly that I want to hear your message." Anything less is an insult to the name of Christ and to the thousands who have been martyred for boldly proclaiming His truth before us! For, the Lamb certainly is worthy for us to live consistent, godly lives.

PART TWO

THE BAPTISM

CHAPTER 5
Baptism

For by one Spirit are we all baptized into one body, whether we be Jews or Gentiles, whether we be bond or free; and have been all made to drink into one Spirit.
— 1 Corinthians 12:13

The Bible teaches that salvation of the soul is always the Lord's doing. No work of the flesh, such as circumcision, attending church, helping people, being good, or even water baptism has ever saved anyone's soul! In Jonah 2:9 of the Old Testament, we read *"Salvation is of the LORD."* In Ephesians 2:8-9 of the New Testament we read that *"For by grace are ye saved through faith; and that not of yourselves: it is the gift of God: Not of works, lest any man should boast."* No one ever has been saved by works. No one! God further explains this in Romans 3:20: *"Therefore by the deeds of the law there shall no flesh be justified in His sight: for by the law is the knowledge of sin."* Praise God for the Law, though. Romans 5:20 teaches us that the Law entered so that the offense might abound. Without the Law we would never have known that we are sinners. God gave us the Law so that we may understand that we are lawbreakers, which means we are sinners. But where sin abounds grace always abounds even more. Galatians 3:21-22 lets us know that the Law never has produced righteousness, but has put us all under sin so that the promise of eternal life can be conferred upon anyone who believes only in the Lord Jesus Christ.

Why Should Christians Be Baptized?

God gives each individual a free will to make choices in life. An individual is saved by God's grace through the choice of his free will by placing his faith in Jesus Christ. An individual chooses to believe the Gospel and wills himself to permit himself to find grace in the sight of God. If we are saved by grace and even when we sin, there is always bountiful grace to forgive our sins. Many ask the question, "Why then should we be baptized after we have received Jesus Christ as our Savior?" The reason is simple. Jesus commanded us to do it. I know that I have repeated this many times in this book, but it is the central theme of the book: The Great Commission. As Jesus was preparing to leave this earth and return to His heavenly domain, He gave His disciples important commissions, or instructions, as to what they were to do. This same great commission applies to all His disciples today as it did around two-thousand years ago. Once again, in Matthew 28:19-20 we read that those commands were *"Go ye therefore, and teach all nations, baptizing them in the name of the Father, and of the Son, and of the Holy Ghost: Teaching them to observe all things whatsoever I have commanded you: and, lo, I am with you alway, even unto the end of the world. Amen."* Jesus commissioned us to (1) *Go*, (2) *Teach all nations*, or all peoples, and (3) *Baptize* these new believers. It is the third commission, to baptize, that is the focus of this chapter. Jesus here challenged his disciples (by the way, if you trust Jesus as your Savior, then you are called to be a disciple of Jesus too) to go unto the world and make disciples or followers and doers of Jesus Christ. The first thing Jesus commissioned His disciples to do was to baptize their new followers. He did not instruct them to first bring them to a thorough understanding of Himself and then baptize them. No. He ordered the reverse. He commissioned His disciples to baptize their new followers and then to (4) *Teach them.*

As you read the book of Acts you will notice that the first step for every new believer of Jesus was to be baptized. They were baptized to outwardly identify without shame that they were followers of Christ to the world. By the way, back then, and even today in some parts of the world, when a believer publicly was baptized to identify with Jesus Christ, he simultaneously made enemies, and enemies who would order them to be martyred. Many of these believers were, and even today are in other countries, martyred for their identification with Jesus Christ. Perhaps we Christians, here in the United States and other comfortable parts of the world, need this type of persecution to bring about a genuine zeal and real dedication to the cause of Christ. I hope it does not have to come to that, but if God so chooses, Amen! We definitely do need a rude awakening of our wickedness among the body of Christ in order to experience a godly repentance.

When we too, as believers, participate in baptism, we are declaring publicly, as these new believers were, that we have placed our faith in Jesus Christ. We are claiming that we now choose to follow Jesus Christ for the rest of our lives. We are unashamedly declaring to the world that we choose to die to our flesh and permit Jesus to reign in our bodies. Accordingly, the first two reasons to be baptized are, first, to be obedient to Jesus Christ's command and, second, to publicly demonstrate our identification with Him to the world.

As I mentioned earlier, the book of Acts is filled with passages of people being saved and then immediately being baptized to prove their faith in the Lord Jesus Christ. The book of Acts is not alone in this biblical way. Being baptized soon after conversion is the pattern in the whole New Testament. This brings up the third reason for why we should be baptized. The New Testament is filled with many other accounts of followers being baptized. Here are a few of the accounts.

In Matthew 3:13-17 we see our first, and prime, example in the New Testament. He is our perfect model. He is the One to whom we look to so that we can learn what we are to do in our own lives. The life of Jesus is the perfect living commentary on what obedience is all about. Jesus Christ's water baptism was His inauguration into His public ministry, and it demonstrated His obedience to carry out the will of God the Father (Hebrews 5:8). His water baptism publicly signified to the world that the mission for the remission of sins of mankind had begun and would be brought forth on this earth. Hallelujah!

Throughout the book of Acts we see many people become followers of Jesus Christ. Their immediate response to their salvation is to identify themselves to Jesus through baptism. Some of the biblical examples who were immediately baptized after belief can be found in Acts 2:41, which shows us where three thousands new believers were baptized the same day. The verse states, *"Then they that gladly received His word were baptized: and the same day there were added unto them about three thousand souls."*

The story of Philip and an Ethiopian eunuch is found in Acts 8:26-39. We read about the eunuch's salvation and his immediate response in Acts 8:35-38. His immediate response after believing on the Lord Jesus Christ for salvation was to get baptized. The verses read: *"Then Philip opened his mouth, and began at the same scripture, and preached unto him Jesus. And as they went on their way, they came unto a certain water: and the eunuch said, See, here is water; what doth hinder me to be baptized? And Philip said, If thou believest with all thine heart, thou mayest. And he answered and said, I believe that Jesus Christ is the Son of God. And he commanded the chariot to stand still: and they went down both into the water, both Philip and the eunuch; and he baptized him."*

The implication of obedience to Christ's command on baptism is at a climax in this passage. This road, from Jerusalem to Gaza, which the Ethiopian eunuch was taking was and still is today a desert. The only water that would have been nearby would have been oasis water.

This means that the eunuch and Philip climbed down into the people's drinking water in order to baptize him. Apparently, Philip and the eunuch both did not think that baptism could wait until a later, more convenient time or area! Additionally, it is noticeable that they did not take a handful of water and sprinkle the eunuch for perhaps sanitary or other reasons. The Bible states that all Philip did was *"preached unto him Jesus"* (verse 35) and then the eunuch said that he wanted to be baptized (verse 36) and he was baptized (verse 38). This means that the preaching of Jesus included advocating the need to be baptized after conversion.

Some other accounts of new believers being baptized immediately after receiving Jesus Christ as their Savior are found in the following: In Acts 9:18, after this encounter with Jesus on the Damascus Road, Saul (later renamed Paul) decided to believe on Jesus as Savior and Lord—and he was baptized. Acts 10:34-48, Cornelius and those with him were commanded to be baptized, becoming the first non-Jewish converts to Christianity that we know of. Acts 16:13-15, Lydia and her household believed and were baptized. In Acts 16:16-34, the Philippian jailer believed and he, along with his household, were baptized—and this was in the middle of the night! Lastly, Paul mentions some names among many people who were baptized after their conversion. In 1 Corinthians 1:13-16 he mentions Crispus, Gaius, and the household of Stephanas. All were baptized in the Gospel of Jesus Christ.

The Bible is clear—belief and baptism are always together. Baptism does not save a person, but baptism always was subsequent soon after persons placed their belief in Jesus Christ for the remission of their sins. Thus, when we believe on the Lord Jesus for salvation, the right time to be baptized is very soon afterwards. If you believed on Jesus for salvation some time ago and were not baptized, then this should become an immediate priority so that you fulfill what God commands and shows you what to do from the Bible.

What Is Baptism?

According to the Thayer's Greek-English Lexicon, the Berry's Interlinear Greek-English New Testament, and in the Strong's Greek Dictionary of the New Testament, the word "baptism" is not an English word. Rather it is an English spelling of the Greek word "baptize," meaning it is a transliteration of the original Greek word baptizw (baptizo). In turn, baptizo comes from the root word baptw (bapto), a term used in the first century for immersing a garment first into bleach and then into dye, both cleansing and changing the color of the cloth. That is an interesting similarity of how God has permitted the usage of the word and the similarity to baptism's cleansing of sin and becoming a new person through Christ. Stated another way, when you process cloth to change its color, you are said to "baptize" it. If sprinkling of any kind was to be practiced, a different Greek word would have been used, but it was not. Baptize means, "to immerse, submerge, to make whelmed." Again, according to the Thayer's Greek-English Lexicon, the Berry's Interlinear Greek-English New Testament, and in the Strong's Greek Dictionary of the New Testament the word "baptize" means to immerse, submerge, and to make WHELMED. The word "whelm" is not found in the Holy Bible. However, the word "whelm" in Noah Webster's 1828 Dictionary means, "to cover with water or other fluid; to cover by immersion in something that envelops on all sides; to cover completely; to immerse deeply."

Therefore, the process of baptism is very simple. You begin by standing, sitting, or kneeling in some water. Another Christian then lowers you completely under the water and then brings you back up out of the water. You could also literally call this "immersion." You are completely immersed in the water. You are not sprinkled, but you are immersed, whelmed, completely covered over all sides underneath water. It is true that some denominations and cults sprinkle water on people instead of immersing them. This practice is not biblical at all because the word baptism has no connotation or any relation or respect to "sprinkle." There are neither illustrations nor teachings to be found in the Bible for Christians to be sprinkled.

Lastly, the erroneous and false idea and practice of sprinkling was never on this planet until it was first introduced around 400 A.D. The religious man, Bishop Augustine of Hippo, Italy, came up with the idea of "original sin." Remember, this man came up with the idea, not the Bible. His idea basically said that everyone inherits the sin of Adam at birth and is therefore separated from God from the beginning of their life, signifying that he discounted God's grace. His teachings meant babies and children were doomed to Hell if they died. This teaching, of course, caused parents to become concerned over the fate of their children, should they die before "getting right with God". Since only one of the four steps required to get right with God could be done by (or to) an infant, they decided, not the Bible, but men decided to baptize their children to "take care of the original sin". Since it is risky to immerse an infant, these people also decided to sprinkle them with water instead— another manmade idea.

This innovation did not become the official practice of the apostate Roman Church until A.D. 1311, when the Council of Ravenna first allowed a choice between immersion and sprinkling. For that reason, these sprinkling ideas are manmade ideas and not God's. The biblical, Christ-centered command of baptism always is by immersion and not by sprinkling water, nor is it for infants.

A saved individual who believes on the Lord Jesus Christ chooses from his own free will to obey the Lord's command to be publicly baptized. Baptism is one of the first "works of righteousness" (Titus 3:5) that a new believer should seek to obey. Again, it is not done to be saved, but to show one's love for the Lord Jesus Christ who has already saved the individual. Galatians 2:16 informs us that a man is not justified by works, but by the faith of Jesus Christ, for works shall not justify any man. Salvation, according to Ephesians 2:8-9, is by grace through faith, not works, lest any man should boast. Baptism is an obedient "work" that is an outward demonstration of one's inward transformation. Baptism is a public statement that we have committed our lives to God. It is a statement expressed in symbolic action as a message to ourselves, to others, and to God. By being baptized, we acknowledge that Jesus is the source of our life and the reason we exist, and that Jesus Christ is our Savior and Lord.

However, many people cannot point to a day and time when they knowingly in their limited human understanding became a Christian. For them, their date of baptism becomes a sort of landmark or type of wonderful memorial in their life that they can look back on and see where God has brought them from and commit to following Him for the rest of their lives. They may not remember when they came to believe on Jesus Christ, but they can remember the day that they publicly demonstrated to the world that they identify with Jesus through their baptism. In that sense, baptism for many people is the second most important landmark and turning point in their lives. The first is the time when we believed and called upon Jesus for salvation.

Baptism has much in common with another ceremony that marks a milestone in many people's lives—marriage. We know how important a marriage ceremony is to the couple in love, as well as to their families and their friends. It is a public statement of their life-long commitment to each other. Certainly, a wedding ceremony does not make a man and woman married in a real sense, though it may do this legally. Neither the ceremony nor its component parts, such as the vows, the pronouncement of the minister or the exchange of rings create the marriage. The commitment and carrying out of that vow to be faithful to each other is what really makes the marriage. Nonetheless, the marriage ceremony is the public statement of the couple's covenant to commit to each other. It is important, although people may also be married without a ceremony.

Baptism pictures the drama of our "I do" decision for Jesus Christ and all that He is in the Plan of Salvation. It is a symbolic act that states we have made a life-long commitment to Christ, believing that He is our Savior. Baptism is our public statement that we will follow Him wherever He may lead us. Those who are obedient to Christ's commandment of baptism are declaring to the world that they want to be associated with Jesus Christ in a personal and intimate way, to belong to Christ, to share in the benefits of His death and life. That is what it means to be baptized "in the name of Jesus Christ."

The Apostle Paul described vividly in Romans 6:3-6 what happens to us believers when we come to Christ to be our Savior. Paul writes, *"Know ye not, that so many of us as were baptized into Jesus Christ were baptized into his death? Therefore we are buried with him by baptism into death: that like as Christ was raised up from the dead by the glory of the Father, even so we also should walk in newness of life. For if we have been planted together in the likeness of his death, we shall be also in the likeness of his resurrection: Knowing this, that our old man is crucified with him, that the body of sin might be destroyed, that henceforth we should not serve sin."* Baptism symbolizes our decision to accept what it means to be united and connected in a relationship with Jesus. Our old nature immediately died along with its desires, wants, will, and passions. Then, according to 2 Corinthians 5:17, in that tinkling of a millisecond, God reformed us and made us into new creatures. All this happens when someone puts his trust in Jesus Christ as Savior. Baptism pictures this reality to the world of what has happened inside a believer. For example, going down into the water symbolizes the death of the self, the immersion of the water symbolizes Christ's blood washing away sins, and the rising up out of the water symbolizes the resurrection of the self to a new eternal life in Christ Jesus.

Of course, baptism is not supernatural. The act of baptism does not mechanically bring the Holy Spirit into us, nor does it cause our spiritual renewal and salvation. Baptism is a ritual, a metaphor that symbolizes that we have died to our former lives and have been reborn to new lives in Christ.

To keep us from thinking about baptism in a supernatural way, we can examine some examples in scripture. First, we have an example where the Holy Spirit did not come immediately to individuals who had been baptized. We read about this in Acts 8:14-17. Many people in Samaria had believed the Gospel and accepted Jesus as Savior. They had also been baptized, but they had not received the Holy Spirit in any noticeable way. In this case, Peter and John later had to place their hands on these individuals and pray for them to receive the Holy Spirit.

In the case of the centurion, Cornelius and his family and friends, the Holy Spirit came before baptism. We learn of this in Acts 10:44-48. They were baptized after receiving the Spirit, but there was no laying on of hands.

The repentant "thief on the cross" could not be and was not baptized at all, yet he was saved.

The first two examples teach us that while baptism is an important public statement of our intentions toward God and Christ, it is symbolic. All three examples teach us that baptism is merely symbolic and does not save someone.

Who Should Be Baptized?

The Bible says there are certain things a person must do before he can be baptized. A person MUST BELIEVE in Jesus Christ with his heart before he can be baptized. If he cannot believe in Jesus Christ then he is not qualified for baptism. Therefore, babies and infants are exempt from baptism. Jesus said in Mark 16:16: *"He that believeth and is baptized shall be saved; but he that believeth not shall be damned.*" Please note that the verse repeats itself and says that he who does not believe shall be damned. Therefore, baptism has nothing to do with justification or righteousness before God. Romans 10:17 teaches us that we come to believe in Jesus as God the Son by hearing the Word of God. The verse states: "*So then faith cometh by hearing, and hearing by the word of God.*" Therefore, a person MUST have faith in Jesus Christ BEFORE he can be baptized. To be baptized before a person believes into Jesus Christ is wrong and ineffective to outward obedience.

A person MUST REPENT before he can be baptized. The Bible in Acts 2:38 says, "*Repent, and be baptized every one of you in the name of Jesus Christ for the remission of sins, and ye shall receive the gift of the Holy Ghost.*" To repent means to have a change of mind. To repent means to feel such sorrow for sin or fault as to be disposed to change one's life for the better (2 Corinthians 7:10). When a person repents he no longer wants to do things his way, but he now wants to do what the Lord Jesus says.

Can a baby repent? Can he change his mind and way of life? No way! Therefore, a baby is not to be baptized!

Before a person can be baptized, he MUST also CONFESS his faith in Jesus Christ. Romans 10:9-10 explains, "*That if thou shalt confess with thy mouth the Lord Jesus, and shalt believe in thine heart that God hath raised him from the dead, thou shalt be saved. For with the heart man believeth unto righteousness; and with the mouth confession is made unto salvation.*" A good example of this is in Acts chapter 8. The man from Ethiopia was being taught by Philip. They came to some water (v. 36). The man from Ethiopia wanted to be baptized. Before Philip baptized him, the Ethiopian man confessed, "I believe that Jesus Christ is the Son of God" (v. 37). After his confession, he was baptized. Baptism came AFTER confession, not before.

Can a baby confess his faith in Jesus Christ as the Son of God? The answer is a definite no! Babies do not understand these truths and they certainly are not able to accurately express their cognitions. They lack a free will. Therefore, a baby is not ready for baptism.

If a Person Was Baptized as an Infant Should That Person Be Re-baptized?

Since biblical baptism is a symbol of what has already taken place in a Christian's heart by placing their faith in Jesus, infant baptism is not a valid baptism. As an infant, you did not make a decision to follow Christ. That is impossible. An infant does not understand that he is a sinner and that he needs Jesus. An infant does not understand that he needs to repent. An infant is not able to accurately communicate any type of cognitions that he may have. Infants lack the understanding of responsibilities and therefore do not yet possess free will. Those individuals who were baptized as an infant and who later in life choose to believe on Jesus for salvation are strongly exhorted to be re-baptized.

Should People Be Re-baptized if They Change Churches or Denominations?

The only reason to be baptized is for a Christian to obey Jesus' command given to us in Matthew 28:19: *"Go ye therefore, and teach all nations, baptizing them in the name of the Father, and of the Son, and of the Holy Ghost."* He said to baptize new believers. Baptism is a symbolic public statement to the world that one declares himself to identify with Jesus Christ and that he has joined himself with the family and community of God and his believers. Baptism is not to declare to the world that you are joining a specific church or denomination. There is no place in scripture to backup that untrue teaching. On the other hand, baptism is a public declaration to the world that you have determined in your heart to believe on the Lord Jesus Christ and that you are going to follow the LORD. The words in Matthew 28:19 clearly instruct us to be baptized *in the name of the Father, and of the Son, and of the Holy Ghost*; not in the name of a church, or a denomination, or a teacher. To be baptized *in the name of the Father, and of the Son, and of the Holy Ghost* is a public acknowledgement that you are submitting yourself under the authority of the LORD and only the LORD. Accordingly, to be baptized in order to join a church or denomination is a man's erroneous and idolatrous idea, and not God's. There are true Jesus believer's in all denominations and probably in every church. The true believers are united and related through the blood of Jesus Christ, not baptism. Our baptism to Christ's command is for a declaration to Him, not to a church.

Does Christ's Command to Baptize Prove the Trinity of God?

Yes, Christ's command to baptize absolutely proves the Trinity of God. It is evidence for the Trinity of God. For Jesus commanded us to baptize *in the name of the Father, and of the Son, and of the Holy Ghost*. Notice that Jesus did not say in the "names," plural. But He commanded, "*in the name*," singular. It was not that He mistakenly said, name. No, He intentionally commanded us to baptize new converts in one name: the name of one God who subsists in three Persons (Father, Son, and Holy Spirit). For each of the three is distinguished from one another; each possess all the divine attributes, yet the three are one.

All Christians will admit that this is a mystery that no analogy can illustrate satisfactorily. God is knowable, yet not discoverable in understanding by human reason. Nonetheless, the illustration that God has given us which probably comes closest to human comprehension and reasoning would be that of the sun, the sunlight, and the power of the sun. Whether we understand the trinity or not, the three Persons are distinguished and are one. We simply need to trust and believe in God in this truth, just as we trust and believe Him to save us, though we are not certain in how His grace accomplishes this.

PART THREE

THE FOLLOW-UP

CHAPTER 6

A Soulwinner Is to Follow-up with Young Christians

But we were gentle among you, even as a nurse cherisheth her children: So being affectionately desirous of you, we were willing to have imparted unto you, not the gospel of God only, but also our own souls, because ye were dear unto us.
– 1 Thessalonians 2:7-8

We have already looked at the first three areas of soulwinning in the Great Commission that Jesus authorized us to do in Matthew 28:19-20: (1) *Go* to the people, (2) *Teach* (tell) the Gospel to the people, and (3) *Baptize* the new converts. These first three areas of the Great Commission certainly bring about great joy when we do them. I must say that there certainly is great joy in going out and telling someone the Gospel and then leading them to Christ. There undoubtedly is great joy in witnessing the new Christian declare his allegiance to Christ through water baptism. Now, we must look even beyond these joyous responsibilities and examine the fourth important responsibility of soulwinning. Do you remember what we are commissioned to do? Christ's Great Commission's fourth responsibility brings about greater joy than the first three combined could ever do. For when the person you have led to Christ grows and develops into a dedicated, fruitful, mature disciple of Christ who then goes on to lead others to Christ and help them in turn, as well—this brings about a marvelous joy that surpasses all of our own joyous labors (3 John 1:4).

This last responsibility is not only amazingly joyous but it is of super great significance. If this last responsibility of soulwinning is not executed, then the whole work of soulwinning will not be successfully accomplished. There is no joy in wasteful labor, for you cannot win the full soul of an individual until you win the individual's full body. This fourth and last commission yields us to continue our involvement in someone's life. We are to continue imparting God's truths into the lives of His new converts and young Christians by investing our time, energy, possessions, resources, and knowledge into them. Without this involvement, the big majority of Christians would not continue and many humans would be despaired from coming into a dynamic love relationship with the Lord Jesus Christ. We must remember that our consideration of strategy, methods, and priorities relating to soulwinning will be incomplete if we do not give much attention to the fourth duty— mentoring and/or disciple making new converts and young Christians. Keep in mind what Jesus ordered us to do at the end of His Great Commission in Matthew 28:20: *"Teaching them to observe all things whatsoever I have commanded you."* This fourth and last commission is directed toward us, as soulwinners, to simply teach His instructive and intimate Word to those whom He has privileged us to lead to the Savior. If we fail to execute this last and very important responsibility of the Great Commission then we are not submitting in obedience to the Lord's command, and this is sin. In this last commission, Christ went a step further than just admonishing us to become disciples. If we are to fall in step with the grand design of God, then we must labor to help people become disciples too. To stop short of that is to fail to capture the genius of the commission of Christ.

Think about this—Jesus asked a very good question in Luke 6:46 that, just like His own twelve disciples, we too need to consider and react to. He asked, *"And why call ye me, Lord, Lord, and do not the things which I say?"* That's a pretty straightforward and powerful question. And, what a subtle, yet, direct rebuke at the same time! Has not the Lord told us within His Great Commission to not only go tell the Gospel to people and to baptize these new converts, but to also teach them His truth? I think so. Therefore, why are so many of us Christians calling Him Lord, yet refuse to get deeply involved in the lives of others? This is hypocritical. Though so many Christians might call Jesus "Lord," and cry out to Him and say, "Lord, Lord," but if they are not investing their time in mentoring or discipling others, then Jesus really is not their Lord. He might be their Savior, but He is not their Lord. They are fooling themselves, and foolishly not subjecting their actions to the obedience of Christ's command. Therefore, it would be wise to do follow-up and get involved into people's lives that He has given us the opportunity to lead to the Savior. It would be a wise thing for us to teach these young Christians the truths that Jesus taught and demonstrated throughout the Holy Bible.

Not only has Jesus commanded us to invest ourselves into the lives of others, but, thankfully, He has also empowered us to accomplish His directive. At another time, Jesus spoke to His disciples and gave them His faithful verbal authorization to do the work of soulwinning. His statement in Luke 10:19-20 empowered them to go out with confidence and accomplish His work on this Earth. He avowed unto them: *"Behold, I give unto you power to tread on serpents and scorpions, and over all the power of the enemy...Notwithstanding in this rejoice not, that the spirits are subject unto you; but rather rejoice, because your names are written in heaven."* As we examine this wonderful, divine declaration, we notice that Jesus was not explaining to His disciples to rejoice because they were given the opportunity to participate in God's work. Nor were they to rejoice because of any successful service that they would experience with God. Although, those things might be good in and of themselves, yet more powerfully He was exhorting them to rejoice because they personally knew God. And as a result of having a relationship with God they now had the awesome privilege to work alongside Him. Just as His disciples needed to understand this, we too surely need to understand this today. Yet, and with great sorrow, it seems to be the opposite today in which most Christians rejoice in. So many Christians rejoice because of the work they see God doing, rather than rejoicing because they have a relationship with Him. It should not be this way. Yes, I agree that it is a joy to see God do a mighty work; however, there should be more joy and rejoicing because our names are written in Heaven.

Unfortunately, many of us have the commercial viewpoint of working to see many souls saved. Then we think, "Thank God... now it is all right." This commercial viewpoint is inadequately incorrect. Our work begins where God's grace has laid the foundation. God's grace lays the foundation of convicting people of their sin and convincing them to call on Jesus for salvation and sanctification in a relationship with Him. We are not to save souls. Actually, we cannot save souls. We are to disciple them. We are to spend our lives and invest our lives into the lives of others. Salvation and sanctification are the work of God's sovereign grace; our work as His disciples is to disciple individuals until they are wholly yielded to God. This might take four years or it might take ten years, but it never happens in one moment, nor one day, nor in a week. One life wholly devoted to God is of more value to God than one million lives simply awakened by His Spirit. As workers for God, we must reproduce His own kind spiritually, and that will be God's witness to us as workers that God has given us success. God brings us to a standard of life by His grace, and we are responsible for reproducing that same holy standard in others.

This spiritual concept of discipling young Christians parallels with nurturing physical newborn babies. After a baby is born in the hospital, the parents bring the baby home. Then, the baby is immediately adorned with care: feeding, bathing, changing diapers, dressing, caressing, and so much more. As the same with a physical newborn baby, we must do the same with spiritual newborn Christians in the Family of God. A new convert is indeed a newborn baby, a spiritual one, I'd like to emphasize. We must immediately attend to his needs regularly and train and teach him the foundational doctrines of the faith such as: assurance of salvation, to profess their new faith to others, to learn to be self-fed from God through being in the Bible and prayer every day, to learn to be attuned to His Spirit, to obey Him, and many other important doctrines. For example, every single time that God privileges me to lead someone to the saving arms of Christ, I immediately spend extra time emphasizing and showing a new convert that he has just engaged into a wonderful relationship with God. I elaborately explain from the Bible that God lives inside of him for the reason for him to know God. I also immediately show him why he needs to be in the Bible every single day. With many new converts, I have made myself available to meet up with them and read the Bible together. I will go to their homes each day or a few times a week, or I will have him meet me at my home or at a park, or just somewhere quiet. Not only do I have the opportunity to genuinely befriend the new convert and love on him, but also during this time together, I have the goal for him to be fed from the Word, and over time my ultimate goal is to help him learn to be directly fed from God. If you and I can get a man to learn to be fed from God, then he will have a better chance of success in the Christian life.

Even God Himself starts to immediately follow-up with new believers through the Holy Spirit. Unlike us, He continues to faithfully work in them for the rest of their lives. God never gives up on someone, unlike you and I can do when we become displeased or hurt by someone. God, with great longsuffering, works in the lives of individuals until He calls them home. The Holy Spirit is the greatest One to follow-up on any one of us and certainly our new converts. You can be sure He does follow-up on each convert. However, this does not excuse a soulwinner from not participating in following-up with a new convert or other young Christians. On the contrary, God has designed new and young Christians to grow through the empowerment and guidance of His Holy

Spirit, the Word, and the involvement of godly people. The Holy Spirit and the Word will teach God's truths. The involvement of a man's life in a young Christian will train God's truths through human participations, practices, experiences, and observations of the Word being lived through another saved individual. So, though the Holy Spirit works to draw young Christians closer to God, this does not mean a soulwinner should not do all he can to assist young Christians to become established and grow in his relationship with Jesus Christ. It is a real comfort to know that those people we meet on airplanes or out of town places, who we may never meet again, will be cared for by the Holy Spirit. Though the Holy Spirit will follow-up with these people, it is our duty to continue to intercede for them through prayer for the rest of our lives. We ought to pray that God will send along devout men and women of God who will disciple them.

CHAPTER 7

The Basis of Investing
Your Life into Others

Since thou wast precious in my [God] sight, thou hast been honourable,
And I have loved thee: therefore will I give men for thee,
And people for thy life.
– Isaiah 43:4

In the biblical pattern of soulwinning, bringing people to a decision for Christ is not the end. Merely, it is the beginning of a marvelous work. When our Lord called the twelve disciples, *"He ordained twelve, that they should be with him, and that he might send them forth to preach, and to have power to heal sicknesses, and to cast out devils"* (Mark 3:14-15). He did not stop with the proclamation of the Kingdom of God or with leading people to choose the Kingdom for salvation. No, He continued and He devoted Himself in the making of disciples. In His Great Commission, Jesus commissioned us to go….and to teach others to observe all things whatsoever He has commanded us. He did not say, "Go and preach only," but He said, *"Go…and teach,"* go make disciples. In Matthew 28:20 Jesus points out how we are to do this disciple making: *"Teaching them to observe all things whatsoever I have commanded you."* You can only teach someone that you have influence over. The more time spent with someone, the more influence you will have in his life. To teach someone can only happen by you giving up your precious time and energy and devoting those resources into the person you are teaching. Time must be spent together developing a friend-to-friend relationship. A lot of practical biblical teaching can and will be involved in the disciple process if you propel your relationship to pass from a teacher-pupil level to an intimate-friendship level. You then will be able to provide a disciple with the maximum amount of aid, when a real friendship is developed where you and he can relate to things along a wide front. This is the critical reason why much time needs to be spent together doing fun things together, laughing together, and crying together. Time must be spent together in the ministry, in each other's homes, in the normal affairs of life, on trips, at work, and at leisure. Time should be spent together in the Word to discuss doctrines, principles, problems, and blessings. Time should be spent together in prayer to unite the hearts of each other together. Discipleship requires that you have a relationship with the total person, not just with his "religious interests."

I can recall one time working with one of my classmates during my college years. He was a baby Christian yet he had a desire to know God more and to do what God has written in His Word. He exemplified himself as an excellent individual to disciple. Though we each had very busy schedules (and to make matters worse, our schedules really conflicted with each other) I knew it would be wise for me to meet up with him and teach him some truths from the Bible. The only free time we found that the both of us could meet up and do some one-on-one devotions together was at 6:00 A.M. in the early morning hours. Since he always had to get up early for some sports practice, it was acceptable with him to meet up with me for an hour once a week. I, on the other hand, disliked getting up so early, but my heart was wanting to see him grow. So once a week I met with him and over that one year's time span I got to make a better friend and what a wonderful privilege it was for me to witness a man grow in the grace and knowledge of Jesus Christ and His Word. Though I lost comfortable sleep, I was rewarded with great joy to see him come to understand certain important biblical truths.

Isaiah 43:4 emphasizes this principle of giving up our lives and devoting them into others in exchange for God to raise up more people to carry on the responsibility. God is speaking in the verse and He proclaims to us: *"Since thou wast precious in my sight, thou hast been honourable, and I have loved thee: therefore will I give men for thee, and people for thy life."* It is marvelous to understand from this verse that we are precious in the sight of the Lord. I do not fully understand the reason. I only gloriously accept it, believe it, and praise Him for that. Then, we gloriously learn that not only does God love us, but He desires to honor our lives by giving us other people in exchange for our lives. The few Christians who choose to stop focusing on their personal lives, and actually get involved in the one or few people around them will be honored by God. Not just honor in Heaven, but He is also speaking of honor here and now on this earth. God honors disciple makers by giving them people, and then more people, in replace of their lives that they have given up. It is sweet to know that each time that we give up our precious time and resources and devote our lives into the life of another person, God promises to honor us by giving us people who will carry on the great work to places that we cannot go.

The reason a soulwinner would make the conscious choice to give up his time, energy, and resources and invest all of that into a life of another individual is because the soulwinner realizes that the life he lives is not his own. For the end of 1 Corinthians 6:19 tells us: *"ye are not your own."* Then the next verse expounds on the reason why we are not our own and then it gives us a command: *"For ye are bought with a price: therefore glorify God in your body, and in your spirit, which are God's."* Then Galatians 2:20 informs us that *"I am* [We are] *crucified with Christ: nevertheless I* [we] *live; yet not I* [we], *but Christ liveth in me* [us]*: and the life which I* [we] *now live in the flesh I* [we] *live by the faith of the Son of God, who loved me* [us]*, and gave himself for me* [us]*."* A disciple maker, whether he knows this verse or not, understands that the life he is living actually is not his own. It belongs to the life of Christ. The Christian is only being privileged to live the life as a steward.

Now that he is a steward, he understands that the best way to use the life that Christ is living through him is to take all of what he has and invest it all into the influence of another life. The disciple maker understands that Christ gave up His life for him and for others, too. Therefore, he is compelled to give up his life for those around him that they may come to know God and do His will too. He is compelled to have a lifestyle in which he cherishes the few individuals that he has the opportunity to work with. Just as 1 Thessalonians 2:20 describes, a soulwinner who is a disciple maker feels deep within his heart an affection that those whom he invests his life into are his glory and his joy unto Jesus Christ. He affectionately and willingly imparts his life into them because they are dear to him. He willingly chooses a sacrificial lifestyle unto others just as Jesus, the Apostle Paul, and many others have demonstrated through their heartfelt actions.

The best individual to analyze, learn, and glean from would be our Lord Jesus Christ. He was the Perfecter in how, why, when, where, and with whom to disciple. Christ set the perfect example of discipleship. However, before we look into His perfect life and superb actions, I would like for us to first visit and look a little into the life of the second greatest disciple maker in the Bible, the Apostle Paul. Don't worry, we will soon enough look closely into the life of Christ and expound in detail on what, how, who, where, when, and why He discipled. For now, let's look a little into the thinking and actions of the Apostle Paul.

The example of the Apostle Paul is uniformly understandable as that set by Jesus. In writing to the Christians in Thessalonica, he expressed his heart by writing: *"But we were gentle among you, even as a nurse cherisheth her children: So being affectionately desirous of you, we were willing to have imparted unto you, not the gospel of God only, but also our own souls, because ye were dear unto us"* (1 Thessalonians 2:7-8). While the Apostle Paul lived on this earth, he realized and demonstrated his belief that he was here to give up his life for others around him. Not only did he not stop with the mere proclamation of the Gospel or with leading people to faith in Christ, but also wherever the Apostle Paul went, he diligently devoted himself in working among the people around him in order to guide them closer to Jesus. As a result, God used him to establish local churches, which became the nerve centers of evangelism within their region. While you and I may not be called to establish big local congregations, we are called to invest our lives into the lives of other believers and eventually support them to start greater awesome new works for the Lord in the lives of other people. There is nothing more winsome than genuine compassion tenderly expressed toward those whom you desire to come closer to Jesus. The Apostle Paul did this very thing. He demonstrated tenderness, love, and affection toward those around him, just as a mother does with her own children. For, outward tender compassion and love is the key to winning the hearts of people. People need to know that they are able to approach us and touch us without fear. Once they know that we are genuine, then they will be apt to follow us and be disciples in the grace of our Lord Jesus Christ.

We can learn a lot more of practical points from the life of Paul. I like one passage of scripture in the Bible, Acts 14:21-23, which provides us with a summary of the methods he used on a consistent daily basis. These verses recapitulate that he and Barnabas preached the Gospel and made many disciples through following-up with these people by visiting them in order to strengthen and exhort them. Then, after he had spent sufficient time in training and teaching them, Paul chose the right leaders from among them to be the continuing leadership of these new churches for new believers. He invested much time in prayer for them often to the Lord. He became their friend and won their trust and respect. He invested his private and public life with them by sharing his time, energy, possessions, and wisdom. For example, we learn in Acts 19:8-10 that while Paul was in Ephesus, he preached in the synagogues for three months regularly. Then, he gathered many believers together and for a time span of two years, he hung out with them, and taught them daily in the school hall of Tyrannus. Please take note that his labor among them was not an overnight, "quick fix" type of work. He invested two years of his life into them. As a result of him taking much time with them, the Gospel spread all over the province of Asia.

The Bible does not isolate discipleship principles only into the books of Acts or in the four Gospels. The Bible is filled with many other examples of men discipling younger men. For example, Elijah discipled Elisha in 1 Kings 19 thru 2 Kings 2; Moses discipled Aaron in Exodus 17 thru Joshua 1; and Eli discipled Samuel in the book of 1 Samuel. We also can see some discipleship principles in the book of 1 John, in particular, that of 1 John 1:3. In this verse John writes about the proclamation of Christ. He writes, *"That which we have seen and heard declare we unto you, that ye also may have fellowship with us: and truly our fellowship is with the Father, and with his Son Jesus Christ."* Let's stop here for a moment. John mentioned something very important. Did you catch why this proclamation was given to us? Let's reread that verse one more time but at a slower pace. The verse again says, *"That which we have seen and heard declare we unto you, that ye also may have fellowship with us: and truly our fellowship is with the Father, and with his Son Jesus Christ."* We learn that the purpose of the proclamation of the Gospel to people is that sinners may begin having fellowship with God and with other believers. Individual conversion is not the ultimate goal of any New Testament soulwinning. It never has been and it never will be. The ultimate objective of the New Testament soulwinning in accordance to the whole Holy Bible is to bring the converted ones into fellowship with God and with each other. The principal step of bringing someone into fellowship is first getting their souls saved. The next lifelong step is working with them to bring them into a dynamic love relationship and fellowship with God and with God's family. I say lifelong step, because, with many people it is a joyous vocation to help them grow in the Word and obedience to God's commands over an extended period of time. I know this personally because, as an example, there is one individual whom I have made myself available to for over a decade now. In the beginning, I sought to build a friendship with the individual. Back then, he was in need of much training and help in knowledge and application of the Word. Today, as I still make myself available to this individual, the man now turns to God first for guidance before seeking man's assistance; one of the areas of growth in his life. That is a great joy for me to witness that type of growth.

During the days of the early first church, it was in this fellowship that mentoring and disciple making of new converts took place. Acts 2:42-46 reveals to us that the Christians had more than their selfish needs on their minds. They were in unity with sharing their food, their possessions, and their lives with one another. This biblical pattern found written all throughout the book of Acts and the New Testament is correctly contrary to the flawed excessive individualism and autonomy that is often seen in our soulwinning efforts in today's churches. Within fellowship, someone can be discipled. With fellowship, there is strength and accountability. Ecclesiastes 4:9-12 says, *"Two are better than one; because they have a good reward for their labour. For if they fall, the one will lift up his fellow: but woe to him that is alone when he falleth; for he hath not another to help him up. Again, if two lie together, then they have heat: but how can one be warm alone? And if one prevail against him, two shall withstand him; and a threefold cord is not quickly broken."* This passage of scripture is a picturesque way of stating a basic principle of life: we need each other. We are not created for isolation, but for fellowship; first with our God, but also with each other in the family of God. Our growth and the growth of young Christians demands fellowship with other Christians, and an important part of that fellowship is accountability; being answerable to others for the conduct of our Christian lives. Our growth and the growth of our young Christians demands not isolation nor individualism, but demands adequate accountability structures where we are hanging out with one another, meeting up with one another, asking and answering the hard questions with one another, and being transparent. This is why James wrote, *"Confess your faults one to another, and pray one for another"* in James 5:16. He was speaking in the lines that we need one another, so much that we must be real and accountable with one another, and with this accountability, we are to love and serve one another.

We Christians desperately need one another, and we would never be able to exist without a little help from our brethren in Christ Jesus. As a disciple maker, there are times when we will want to be alone with our disciple and to help him in various areas of his life in a private setting. However, we should not always meet disciples in private settings. We should never have the idea, as a disciple maker, that you and I are the only "life line" that our disciple needs to learn from. If we do this, we will be making a mirror image of ourselves, and this is idolatry. This is not good. Each one of us has weaknesses, struggles, and deficiencies and we certainly would not want our disciples to become like us with the same weaknesses, struggles, and deficiencies.

We are never to attempt to make anyone to become exactly like ourselves. This is one reason why Jesus instituted the collective body of believers in the church. The church is like an incubator for believers. Though we may disciple individuals, we should let them have their freedom to gain insight, knowledge, and wisdom through their self-choice of who they will be influenced by and hang out with. Then, no carbon copying of ourselves will be happening; instead, a pricking of their heart through different relationships will provoke them to become as Christ.

Though I have just warned why we should not isolate a disciple from others, I am afraid that this may not be the real problem with most churches today. It seems that most churches today have turned themselves to the other extreme, which is an equal killer for baby Christians as the other is. This modern day autonomy isolation through the week, and "hello, see you at the next church service" Christianity is an unbiblical and an ineffective fellowship that can never produce a disciple. The Bible is so much against this new modern day isolation disservice to one another, that to prove this point I am going to give a list of scriptures that depict and instruct us toward fellowship with one another, not isolation! It is found all over the New Testament, but for time's sake, here is a short list from some hundreds of references: Acts 2:42-47; 20:7; Romans 12:10,13, 16; 15:7, 14; 1 Corinthians 12:7; Galatians 6:2; Ephesians 4:3, 16; 5:19; Colossians 3:16; 1 Thessalonians 5:11; Hebrews 3:13; 10:24; and James 5:16.

Disciples can only be made with first being a friend to someone, helping their physical life in certain capacities, and imparting and teaching them the Word of God faithfully on a regular basis. When Christians meet together in most churches today, they have transformed themselves into unbiblical centers of organizations because the industrial/business model for organizations is influencing them. Not only that, but they are consumed with efficiency and bureaucracy as their hallmarks. To make matters worse, they are not devoted to the Word, nor enthusiastic about the well-being of another's soul, but instead they are obsessed with carrying out and multiplying more and more activities, organizations, and committees; relegating people into some program hoping that it will do an adequate job for them. Meanwhile, vital relationships are lost or completely ignored in the process and new converts are fragmented into age-segregated and functional subgroups as soon as they walk in a church door. This should not be! It is unbiblical (1 Corinthians 10:24). As a result the hope of adequacy is out the door and deficiency is now inside.

We Christians ought to reexamine how Jesus invested his time and life into the lives of people around Him while He was down here on this earth. Jesus never once segmented people around him into groups based on age, gender, personalities, or interests. In fact, Jesus never segmented anyone. He welcome the loud little children into His arms and lap while teaching people important truths (Matthew 19:14). He welcomed sinners and the righteous together as He talked with them (Luke 15:1-2).

We would do ourselves a whole lot of good if we would diligently search the stories of the Bible and reexamine the biblical methods and principles of follow-up. For example, notice how Paul worked with people. Acts 17:17 lets us know that he was glad to work with people of different groups together. As we reexamine the scriptures we will discover that our modern day methods are frail, weak, and unbiblical. They are crippling Christians instead of enabling them. If we reexamine our ways and compare them to the ways and methods of Christ and the New Testament, we might even awaken to revive our ways and truly sacrificially invest our lives into the individuals around us. On that last note, I must yell, "Hallelujah," in hopes that we will do such things.

CHAPTER 8

There Is a Great Need

Then saith he [Jesus] unto his disciples, The harvest truly is plenteous, but the labourers are few; Pray ye therefore the Lord of the harvest, that he will send forth labourers into his harvest.
– Matthew 9:37-38

While Jesus looked over his shoulders and observed the mass crowd around Him, He turned to His disciples and said to them in Matthew 9:37-38: *"The harvest truly is plenteous, but the labourers are few; Pray ye therefore the Lord of the harvest, that he will send forth labourers into his harvest."* Here Jesus saw the desperate sight for the need of more laborers to rise up and labor among the people.

Just as back then, today, there certainly is a great need for more soulwinners to rise up and invest their lives into the lives of others. Not only guiding people to Christ for salvation, but also, the need of spending quality time with young Christians in guiding them even closer to the Savior and His Word more, so, that they too can intimately know Him and get involved in the great work of soulwinning. Following-up with young Christians is very much needed to conserve the fruits of soulwinning. Follow-up can only happen through the mentoring and/ or disciple making of young Christians, though. The weakest area of modern day soulwinning efforts is to do disciple making and at the very minimal to mentor young Christians. The labor of mentoring and disciple making in today's churches is so feeble that it is practically unobserved in the majority of churches today. This is pathetic and sorrowful! Nonetheless, I do praise God that thousands and thousands of people out of the billions of people around the world do respond to the invitation and make a personal decision for salvation. But, and it's a big BUT, depressingly there are only a very small number of these thousands who really have the privilege to be followed-up on and discipled in order to become disciples and effectual soulwinners themselves, instead of mere believers on the Lord Jesus Christ. Remember, Jesus established the fact in John 8:31, John 13:35, John 15:8, and Acts 14:22 that He came to make disciples, and not mere believers.

When you and I read the Gospel of Luke and the other three Gospels, we will notice something striking about the way Jesus calls for commitment unto Himself. Jesus never calls for vague interest or half-hearted or even individuals with 95% interest to be followers of Him. No. Jesus is far more radical in His call for disciples. Jesus wants people to put all their hopes, all their interests, all their beliefs, and all their plans and service in dedication to follow Him. For example, in Luke 9:23 Jesus warned us that if anyone desires to come after Him, that individual must take up his cross daily, and follow Him. Jesus is searching for disciples who will deny everything about themselves and authorize Him to have absolute control of every area of their lives. Then, later in the chapter, Jesus gave us the criteria in order to be His disciples who would be valued worthy to go make other disciples. In Luke 9:57-62 the passage reads: *"And it came to pass, that, as they went in the way, a certain man said unto him, Lord, I will follow thee whithersoever thou goest. And Jesus said unto him, Foxes have holes, and birds of the air have nests; but the Son of man hath not where to lay his head. And he said unto another, Follow me. But he said, Lord, suffer me first to go and bury my father. Jesus said unto him, Let the dead bury their dead: but go thou and preach the kingdom of God. And another also said, Lord, I will follow thee; but let me first go bid them farewell, which are at home at my house. And Jesus said unto him, No man, having put his hand to the plough, and looking back, is fit for the kingdom of God."* In this passage of scripture, Jesus warned us Christians of three criteria in order to be His disciples and have the privilege to go out and make more disciples for His Kingdom. Those three criteria are a big cost; we must consider and be willing to sacrifice and abandon from our lives at anytime in order to make disciples. Those three criteria are costs in our personal comfort; costs in our time, especially the time of "now;" and costs in our priorities.

If you or I are going to be involved in the lives of people, if we are going to invest our lives into the lives of others, and if we are going to disciple people in order to bring them closer to Jesus, then we must understand and decide that if there is any comfort in this work, the only comfort is the willingly cherishing and affectingly imparting of our lives into the few lives of people around us (1 Thessalonians 2:7-8). There is really usually no comfort in this vocation other than that. We must willingly and cheerfully surrender our perceived comforts (others might like to say pleasures). I say perceived comforts or pleasures because once we start to willingly surrender our lives unto people around us, we soon learn that our once perceived comforts and pleasures are really not that important; and God enlightens us with new more wonderful comforts and pleasures through unique experiences. For example, many times a disciple maker will be called to help someone when it seems to not be the best convenient time or when it does not feel comfortable. I know this firsthand because I once was at home taking care of some things and enjoying the day all to myself, when all of the sudden in the middle of what I was doing, I received a phone call from a young man that I was investing my life into. He told me that he needed a ride and requested if I could go pick him up and take him to another location. There was just one small additional inconvenience—he was located clear across town! However, I thought about what I was doing and considered his need. I realized that what I was presently doing could be delayed until another time and that his need was an opportunity that could become great training in servant hood and time alone in a car with him so that we could fellowship and talk about the Word together. I ended what I was doing and drove clear across town, picked him up, and took him to the place he needed to be. Meanwhile, we had a great time in the car ride together; he was able to witness servant hood with joy complete, and we had good conversation about the Word and personal talk. The moral of my example is that if you and I are going to mentor or disciple another person, then we must perceive and value our lives literally as a doormat for others if we are going to have any success in discipling young Christians. We must quietly live to be a "Welcome Sign" for people to use us in any way for their benefit and verbally guide them to come closer to Christ. Another lesson of the story is that what I at first perceived to be an inconvenience actually turned out to be a wonderful experience and memory of him and I together in the car. Our perceived comforts and pleasures are not what they always seem to be. God many times just might want to give us a unique experience with someone, but we have to be willing to sacrifice our personal comforts to receive the benefits and long-lasting rewards.

Servant hood was a prime characteristic of Jesus. Matthew 20:28 shows us that *"the Son of man came not to be ministered unto, but to minister, and to give his life a ransom for many."* As Jesus always demonstrated this characteristic, the same is a necessary quality for a disciple maker to have in his life. He will oftentimes have to subject himself to the service of others. This is expected of a godly disciple maker. Therefore, his basic attitude has to be that of John the Baptist, who said of Jesus, *"He must increase, but I must decrease"* (John 3:30).

Being willing to be a disciple maker and surrendering our personal comfort comes with the attitude that we must be willing to spend and to be spent for the benefit of others (2 Corinthians 12:15). We cannot complain. We cannot murmur. Our own "rights" must diminish as we serve others. This is the reason why Jesus taught in Mark 10:43-44 that we ought to view our life with a humble sense of servant hood, with a humble sense that we have no value except for Christ to be honored and for others to be benefited through our expense. This is why if we are going to be disciple makers we must have an attitude like a slave. Meaning, slaves acknowledge and know for a fact that their opinion (Proverbs 18:2) and their own desires and "rights" (Luke 9:23) do not matter one bit. They quite well understand that the only opinion, desires, and rights that matter are that of their master. We Christians have a Master and His name is Jesus the Christ. Jesus is the Master and His Word matters and His desire for young Christians to be helped is what only matters. Not what we think matters. If you or I live our lives with a mentality of a slave, then when someone needs help, we will make ourselves available to be used in service to them for the edification of bringing them closer to God. A disciple maker must be available to his disciple constantly. His life must be deep in his own fellowship with Jesus Christ so that his life might be a focal point for the Holy Spirit to use as a means of being an example to his disciple.

Jesus, in Luke 9:57-62, informed us of the second criteria in order to be a soulwinner who makes disciples: the costs of "now." Meaning, we must understand and appreciate that our time is not our time. All time that we use and enjoy, each second is lent to us from God. We are only borrowing it. The time we use is God's time and it is to be used with good stewardship to glorify Christ in whatever we do. We are to use our time in the service of others for their benefit in coming closer to God. For example, I have gotten up out of bed at two in the morning to listen and talk to a man I was discipling. He much needed someone to listen to him and though I wanted sleep, I knew the sacrifice was more important than my personal comfort. Therefore, if someone calls you at three in the morning, you, as a disciple maker should have the attitude that though it is not comfortable to talk to them because you are sleepy, you should still have the attitude to get up and listen to their great concern and even perhaps serve them in any other needed ways. May we, and I say WE because I am guilty of this too, may we not be found any longer in robbing God of His time with our selfish desires and wants, when He is giving us an opportunity and privilege to serve someone when we think it is not most convenient or comfortable. The service in people's lives will most generally occur when we least expect it and more than often at the most inconvenient times. This is part of being a soulwinner who is willing to make disciples in the Kingdom of God.

Lastly, Jesus mentioned the third criteria in order to be a soulwinner who makes disciples; that is to have your priorities correct. How important this criterion is! Jesus will only impart His great work of discipleship into the lives of those Christians who have their priorities correct. God is not going to send baby Christians to Christians with wrong priorities so that these young Christians can be trained in destructive habits. No. God will only send young Christians to the soulwinners who have their priorities aligned to His priorities. Our priorities should be first to seek God and His righteousness (Matthew 6:33), then our family (1 Timothy 5:8), and finally others (Philippians 2:4)—not our own lives, not our jobs, nor our personal things. Our jobs, possessions, personal lives, and other responsibilities do not even fit in the list of priorities. These are all secondary. These items are secondary and do not fit in the priority list because they are tools for us to use in His service. God has permitted us to have them so that they can be the useful tools that He chooses to use to support His work through us. For example, God permits Christians to work and earn money in life. The biblical priority of work is not to earn money in order to take care of our personal needs. The biblical priority of work is to earn money for whatever He wants, ministry. If we would work and seek Him for what He wants, He will reveal how we can minister through that job and perhaps even use the money for His Kingdom, too, and lastly to take care of our personal needs. All things God permits us to have and be part of are given to us for three reasons: that we may know Him more, to serve others, and to use our resources for His working in the ministry of others.

All too often, so many Christians fool themselves and think that they are doing God a great service because they came up with an idea on their own and are doing it in "His Name," yet their priorities are not right. I am afraid that Christians like this will find themselves with little to no reward in Heaven. We are to seek God and do His will. Not our will, even if we all too often label it as a "Christian" thing. This is why God warns us in Ephesians 5:17, *"Wherefore be ye not unwise, but understanding what the will of the Lord is."* We are commanded not to be ignorant of what the will of the Lord is. We are commanded to understand what the will of the Lord is. The will of the Lord is that men may come into having a knowing-fellowship with Him, according to John 6:40 and John 17:3. That can only happen with the Word, the Holy Spirit, and the involvement of men's lives into the life of another. God will not impart His true work of disciple making into someone's life until their priorities are aligned to His priorities. God refuses to allow anyone to rob Him of His glory (Isaiah 42:8). God abhors seeing religious people making other religious people. This is why Jesus warned us in Matthew chapter 15, in particular to verse 14, to have our priorities correct so that we will not be like the religious leaders of His day and guide the blind from one incorrect path to another incorrect path. God only calls the few soulwinners who have their priorities aligned to His will to be elevated to disciple young Christians.

Since most Christians look at these costs of discipleship and reject them, most Christians never will have the privilege to disciple another man. Most look at the costs and say, "Ahh, that's too hard. That's too much to give up." And so, God graciously lets them still be part of the Family of God, but unfortunately, they reject God's many blessings offered in the Family and they will never receive the joys and the uncountable blessings that come along with investing their lives into someone else's. Unfortunately, this is the reason why the mass majority of new young Christians are left alone to fall away and never come into a deep meaningful relationship with the One who paid the heavy price and saved them. Again, that is pathetic and disheartening. It breaks the heart of God. Even so, God will righteously judge the pride and self-centeredness of Christians who refuse to prioritize Him first and put people before themselves.

The lack of discipling and mentoring taking place in today's churches is loyal disobedience to the fourth commission in Jesus' Great Commission found in Matthew 28:20. This disobedience is one of the reasons why God is restraining His power as He would have it flow through us into the world. Revelation chapters 2 and 3 severely admonish us by showing God's capabilities in disciplines and reprimands concerning those Christians who refuse to operate in His Kingdom through His established methods and principles; such as the commissioned principle to mentor and disciple.

There are also those young Christians who are dropouts in spite of our best "modern day" follow-up methods and literature. The reason is often that neither the church nor the individual Christians share any responsibility in following-up with young Christians. Follow-up should not be pushed onto any other organization. Mentoring and discipling young Christians are the work of the church. May I remind you, the church is not a building either. The church is the body of Christ, which is only made up of individual Christians (Ephesians 1:22-23). These individuals are to collectively come together in order to spur one another to greater works so that they can go out, do the work of reconciliation and invest their time, energy, possessions, and lives into the lives of new individual Christians. If you are part of the church, the body of Christ, meaning you are a born again believing Christian, then you must take it upon yourself to invest your time into the life of someone else outside of the church building or outside of some Christian organization.

A new believer is often very alert and eager to learn new spiritual truths and take fresh steps of obedience. He is eager to listen to any teaching that supposedly comes from the Bible. His new eagerness and zeal is what makes him a target for false teachings and cults. If he is not taught and trained in the truth and sound doctrines, then his soul will not be satisfied and his hunger may be misdirected.

Another point is that mentoring and discipling is very essential in order to make strong, balanced, witnessing Christians out of new believers. Many excited new Christians are sometimes tragically led into some unimportant minor subjects as a focus in their new life. As a result, the baby Christians become unbalanced in their Christian life and witness. They then begin to ignorantly emphasize those biblical teachings, which should only be peripheral, and they neglect to focus on the biblical basics and foundational doctrines, which should be the central focus of their passions and zeal. For the basic doctrines are foundational for this very point: Foundations are laid for strength, structure, and guidance in all other truths. Foundational truths are the landmarks in the build up and the establishment of other biblical doctrines and truths. However, the reason for this error is because they have a lack of balanced Bible teaching and training. Or, they may continue living a self-complacent, fruitless life which lacks personal involvement and charity. This is because as Christians they are not taught from the Bible nor trained through personal experience in what their privileges, responsibilities, and resources are. This is a sad tragedy to see so many Christians who meet week after week in some wonderful fellowship to sing choruses and praises to God, listen to sermons, and then sadly go about totally indifferent to the needs of their fellowmen around them during the week, and never make any impact on them! This should never be, yet it is happening all over today.

The soulwinner that is disciplined to mentor or disciple other Christians will labor, reach out, and work to see life's relationships grow to become full of divine potential. This is, above all, a dangerously enlarged giving heart. Its high ideals and expanded sympathies make it susceptible to a list of sorrows unknown to a small self-centered heart, but it is also open to a volume of joys and pleasures that the shriveled self-centered heart will never even be able to imagine.

As I stated earlier, we Christians ought to reexamine how Jesus invested his time and life into the lives of people around Him while He was down here on this earth. We ought to seek the passages of the Bible and reexamine the biblical methods and principles of follow-up, and as we reexamine the scriptures, we will discover that our modern day methods are frail, weak, and unbiblical. There is a great need out there for young Christians to be mentored and discipled. There is a dire need out there and within our local congregations for you and me to faithfully make the time, use our energy, and faithfully get involved into the lives of some hungry Christians around us on a regular basis. Jesus surely was not wrong when he stated to His disciples in Matthew 9:37-38: *"The harvest truly is plenteous, but the labourers are few; Pray ye therefore the Lord of the harvest, that he will send forth labourers into his harvest."* May we reexamine and meditate on this passage of scripture, and may our hearts be overwhelmed with conviction to go out and get involved in another person's life.

CHAPTER 9

The Differences Between Discipling and Mentoring

And the things that thou hast heard of me among many witnesses,
the same commit thou to faithful men, who shall be
able to teach others also.
– 2 Timothy 2:2

Christians can lead a soul to Christ within a few minutes to a couple hours, but it takes more than that to bring someone into a dynamic fellowship with God. Remember, soulwinning involves more than proclaiming the Gospel and guiding someone to Jesus for salvation. Soulwinning also involves taking your life and investing it into the life of another Christian through mentoring or discipling someone over an extended period of time. Most generally, when you and I get involved in someone's life it is for the long haul, meaning years, perhaps even decades. God promises to us in Isaiah 43:4 that He will exchange our lives for the lives of others when we give Him our lives through the involvements and investments of our time, energy, and resources into other lives around us. This can happen either through mentorship or discipleship. Many Christians have a blurred understanding about the differences between mentorship and discipleship. They both seem the same. It also can appear that the two are the same or that they are intertwined and mixed together. However, there is a distinction between mentoring and disciple making. If someone should break both down and explain them in their most basic and fundamental explanation, an individual can sum each one in one word; mentoring is teaching and disciple making is training.

Mentoring is designed to empower the protégé (a baby or young Christian) by ways of guiding or pointing his thinking process towards that of the Word and God's will. This is accomplished through well-crafted questions, feedbacks, and challenges through meetings that the young Christian can receive and think about and ponder on. For example, if I am mentoring a younger man I might ask him to spend some time thinking about, "How do God's desires and wants differ from what he desires and wants about a particular interest at hand?" Mentoring may involve times when the mentor teaches and explains truth from the Bible to the young Christian. The young Christian listens as in-depth teaching or instruction is given about a particular principle or truth from the Bible. The young Christian may ask questions and the mentor either will answer the questions or will propose feedbacks and challenges to the young Christian. Mentoring is all done in a friendly and two-way relationship backed-up by trust. Mentoring bonds may linger for a few days or continue a lifetime, as far as the two parties believe that the process should carry on.

In comparison to the processes of mentoring which include guiding the young Christian into a new, godly way of thinking using conversations, teachings, and meetings; disciple making goes a lot deeper. Discipleship is making someone to look like the other. The second greatest disciple maker, the Apostle Paul, understood this principle. He humbly repeated this notion throughout his writings:

1 Corinthians 11:1—*"Be ye followers of me, even as I also am of Christ."*
Philippians 3:17—*"Brethren, be followers together of me, and mark them which walk so as ye have us for an ensample."*
Philippians 4:9—*"Those things, which ye have both learned, and received, and heard, and seen in me, do: and the God of peace shall be with you."*

2 Thessalonians 3:9—*"Not because we have not power, but to make ourselves an ensample unto you to follow us."*

This notion, "to follow another," is an important factor in discipleship. Any disciple maker who is following Christ can say and do as Paul did. It requires great humility to exemplify Christ before another so that they should observe and do as you do. This is why Paul had no hesitation in instructing his disciples to do as he was doing. Paul had set himself up to be an example for people to follow because he was following Christ.

This comes with a caution, though. A bad disciple maker will make a bad disciple. A godly disciple maker will make a godly disciple. A bad disciple maker attempts to make a follower to become like himself. A godly disciple maker attempts to ultimately make a follower to look like Jesus. This caution is the reason why disciple makers need to be following Christ or not disciple at all. On the other hand, I have heard some older, well-versed Christians give an excuse of why they should not disciple. Nonetheless, their excuse still does not relieve any one of us from the duty of discipling people. They say, "Well, now, I don't want people following my example; I'd rather they follow Christ's example." Who wouldn't prefer that? I know I would. However, there is a big problem underlining their statement. Our disciples will not follow Christ's example, at least, not at the beginning of their walk with the Lord. A baby Christian's concept of "following Christ" is too abstract for them. A baby Christian possesses little to no understanding of their new Savior and they are zealously interested in the trivial concerns of how a real flesh-and-blood Christian looks, acts, and reacts. They are unaware of the deeper concerns of the heart in "following Christ". As Christopher Adsit writes in his book, *Personal Disciplemaking: A Step-by-step Guide for Leading a Christian From New Birth to Maturiy* on pages 83 and 84: " 'They want to know how [our] spiritual life functions, what [we] do, what works for [us], [our] fears and hopes. That fleshes it out for them and encourages them that following Christ can be done, or that they aren't the only ones who struggle.' Just as a real-life child looks up to and imitates his parents, so your disciple will copy you at first. He'll accept a great deal of what you accept and he'll leave out much of what you leave out."

Until the day comes when he exemplifies you and starts to point his questions, concerns, focus, and attention to Jesus, the real question that you should be asking is not whether you should be an example to him— The question should be whether you will be a good example or a bad one. In either case, you are going to be making a significant impression on your disciple. May you, therefore, choose to exemplify a life that focuses on Christ and does as Christ does (1 John 2:6).

To say it a different way, mentoring is an arrangement where the young Christian is mentored to learn principles and truths in getting to know God and serving God more effectively and more obediently. Disciple making is an arrangement where the young Christian is discipled to become like the person whom he is being discipled. Unlike mentoring, where the mentor and the young Christian only meet up sometimes for meetings or teachings, discipleship involves the disciple maker permitting and making ways for the disciple to hang out all the time with him. The disciple maker permits the development of the disciple to become more intimate and permit a deep friendship to be evolved while training the disciple to observe what he does and does not do in life's experiences; meanwhile always referring back to the Bible for truths and corrections. Discipleship basically is friendship with a long-term vision for the one you care. If the disciple is being discipled by a godly individual, then the young Christian will be discipled to look and do, or imitate, as the disciple maker, and ultimately the young Christian will be transformed inside to be conformed to the Principal Discipler— Jesus Christ. This is why Paul could say to those in Philippi: *"Those things, which ye have both learned, and received, and heard, and seen in me, do.*" because he was a man that followed Christ and exemplified Christ. A man who is following Jesus will make other disciples who will follow Jesus (1 Corinthians 11:1). He will invest his life into the young Christian to seek out what Jesus wills, what Jesus did, what Jesus said, and where Jesus went. All about Jesus!

As a personal example, I will make myself available many times to many people who desire to be mentored by me. I will let them come over to my home or take a car ride with me so I can accomplish my mundane tasks, meanwhile being a servant to them. On the other hand, I never give myself to the many for discipleship. I only give myself to the few. I only make myself available to personally spend much time, energy, and resources into the few that able themselves to be discipled. The few that I choose to invest much of myself into must be men who demonstrate that they are faithful, available, teachable, and trainable. [You can remember these four important qualities by remembering the acronym FATT (**F**aithful, **A**vailable, **T**eachable, **T**rainable).] These qualities are derived from the instructions found in 2 Timothy 2:2: "*And the things that thou hast heard of me among many witnesses, the same commit thou to faithful men, who shall be able to teach others also.*" What I mean by these four qualities is in being faithful, an individual shows himself over a chosen period of time to be constant and consistent in his performances of personal responsibilities and services. For example, does he consistently spend time with God every day in the Bible? Does he consistently follow through with duties, obligations, requests, or services? You will want an individual who shows himself to be a "yes" answer to both of these questions. An available individual is one who makes himself ready and available so that he can spend quality time with you. An individual who is teachable is one who is eager to learn. He does not have a presumptuous attitude, but instead is submissive to listen and hear the Word of God and principles taught to him. An individual who is trainable is one who is able to assimilate what you share with him through teachings and personal examples.

If I am going to invest much of myself into someone, then my hope is that they will reproduce what I am instilling into them, so that years down the line I can receive the joy of witnessing them investing their lives into the lives of others (3 John 1:4). If a man is not faithful, available, teachable, or trainable, then he demonstrates higher potential of not successfully using his life to accomplish the Great Commission, a lifelong investment in the lives of others around him. Such an individual, I do not judge or condemn him, but I indeed pray for him. Whenever such an individual comes around me, I will keep myself available for him to hear encouragements, exhortations, and admonishments from God's Word. In the long run, hopefully he will choose to allow God to work inside him so that He can ready himself to rise up and eventually become trained to be a successful Matthew 9:38 laborer.

This may sound harsh, and quite frankly it is; and, I understand that this is a touchy issue with some people, but how can you and I follow in Jesus' steps if we do not make a stab at figuring out what He did? 1 John 2:6 says, "*He* [Speaking about you and I] *that saith he abideth in him* [Jesus] *ought himself also so to walk, even as he walked.*" Jesus realized that time is a very precious asset. Jesus made Himself available to all people, but He only invested His life into the faithful. Therefore, if Jesus only invested the entirety of Himself into the few faithful, then you and I need to do as He did, or we are going to find ourselves failing at disciple making, and eventually becoming frustrated, disgruntled, and giving up. Again, time is a precious asset and life is too short to try to be chasing around and trying to encourage all the Christians who do not really have a desire to be about the things of God. Since we only have twenty-four hours in a day and since we only have one life to live, we cannot afford to waste time. This means that we must make sure that the people to whom we give our lives are the right ones: those who are faithful, available, teachable, and trainable. We must make sure that what we teach and train them actually meets their needs, or then we will be wasting both of our times, and that is a disservice and not discipleship. Second Timothy 2:2 instructs us not to waste our time with such apathetic or lackadaisical individuals. We are to leave them to God. He can work with them and prepare them to hopefully and eventually become faithful, available, teachable, and trainable for a future time. So, for the present time, we need to apply the wise instruction for us to be selective with whom we are going to fully impart and invest all of our life into, and those select few need to be what Jesus looked for in individuals—FATT people!

Jesus perfectly modeled discipleship while He was on this earth. Matthew 7:29 reads, *"For he* [Jesus] *taught them as one having authority, and not as the scribes."* My opinion does not really matter, but I think one reason Jesus taught with authority was because <u>He did the things He taught</u>. There are many Christian leaders who preach great sermons, but are not actually involved with evangelism, following-up with young Christians, discipling hungry people, or training those who want to become a laborer! They will have authority as a teacher but not as a trainer. Yet, Jesus did both! Jesus set the pattern and method of disciple making through His life of teaching and training in order to exemplify to us that we need to do both; and how we can accomplish His work successfully.

In John 3:16 we learn that Jesus loved the whole world. In Mark 8:9 we learn that Jesus helped the thousands. He always helped those who were in need. He had an influence in their lives. Nonetheless, Jesus realized that it was humanly impossible to invest His life, time, and energy into the multitudes. As you read the Gospels, you will notice that Jesus always made Himself to be available to anyone. This is significant. Anyone was allowed to come and hang around Jesus and listen to His teachings and be influenced in the midst of the training of the few. Nevertheless, out of the multitudes of people around Him Jesus only trained the faithful!

We learn in Luke 10:1 that Jesus narrowed His attention and He chose seventy men who distinguished themselves in demonstrating that they were faithful. These seventy men were permitted to be discipled by Him from a short distance. These men in the Gospels were around Jesus quite more often than the multitudes. The multitudes are noticed to be made of many types of people who would come and go. The seventy were a group of men who stayed around, hung around, and learned from Jesus all the time. They had an influence from the life of Jesus. They were given tasks to do, He would send them out to do them, and they learned some of the work of ministry. However, Jesus had great understanding. He understood that it still would be humanly impossible to invest all of His life, time, and energy into a group of seventy men.

So, we notice in Luke 6:13-16 that Jesus narrowed more of His focus onto twelve men. We learn from the four Gospels that Jesus spent much time with these twelve men. He focused on them much more through investing his time, energy, instructions, teachings, and training into their lives. He gave a great deal of Himself, including privacy and public life to them. The method of discipleship Jesus demonstrated in His relationship with these twelve did not include enrolling His disciples in a classroom course and addressing only their minds. No, He chose them, *"that they should be with him"* (Mark 3:14); and they talked, worked, walked, ate, and slept together for around three and a half years. He allowed them very close to Himself all the time so that they could learn by watching, listening, and doing as Jesus taught them, and modeled for them; Jesus established them in God's truths, He equipped them and trained them in the life God wanted them to live.

Once again, Jesus understood that it would be humanly impossible to give all of His time, energy, and all of Himself into the twelve. He understood that it would be humanly impossible to thoroughly disciple and successfully equip so many men for what they needed. Therefore, He narrowed His focus even more into the lives of three of them: Peter, James, and John. We learn in Luke 9:28 that Jesus zeroed in on these three men. With these three men, we see in the four Gospels that <u>Jesus gave ALL of Himself to the very few</u>—these three men. He gave all of His time, energy, teachings, and training. He always taught and trained them in the presence of others; the multitudes, the seventy and the other nine disciples. Then also, we see in the Gospels that sometimes Jesus took these three men aside and devoted special private times of revelation and teaching, instruction, and training. For example, He shared great experiences with them by permitting them to see His Transfiguration, to see Him resurrect Jairus' daughter, and witness His sorrow in Gethsemane. Jesus built a great intimate relationship with these three men, and therefore was able to make them to be better equipped and to be more focused disciples for His mission on this earth.

Jesus knew that it is not humanly possible to invest oneself into a large number of people, but that it is humanly possible to invest all of oneself into the lives of the few. That is what He exemplified before us so that we feeble humans would know how to correctly and successfully multiply and propagate His mission.

Yet one more note—out of all the people Jesus allowed around Himself, out of the few people Jesus allowed to be close to Him, we learn in John 21:15-19 that Jesus entrusted the ministry into the life of one man, Peter. There comes a time when we will have to narrow all of ourselves, possessions, time, teachings, wisdom, knowledge, and everything into one individual so that he can be the one who we can entrust our ministry over to in the future when we will be gone.

The discipleship model that Jesus gave us through His example can be explained to you in words, as I just attempted to do. However, all of what I have just explained to you can be illustrated in a diagram. Some of us are better at reading and understanding something, and others of us are better at seeing an illustration and visually understanding a truth. The following diagram after this paragraph is an illustration that depicts Jesus' method of how to successfully disciple people around us. I encourage you to study this out and implement Christ's method into your personal life too. If you live your life by the method that Jesus lived His life, you will in the long-run find God's work to be more successful, more rewarding, more joyful, and more fruitful. You will find in the long-run that God will multiply your life and your work for Him over and beyond what you could ever imagine, for God clearly did inform us of that in Isaiah 43:4. We just have to use biblical principles and Jesus' methods to accomplish and see God multiply our lives in a great degree beyond what any of us could ever attempt to do on our own. Discipleship is this Isaiah 43:4 door to multiplicity. It is my sincere hope for you that will yield your life to the methods that Jesus utilized while He was down here on the earth.

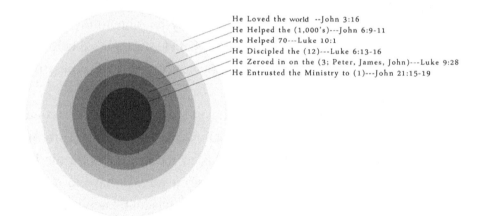

He Loved the world --John 3:16
He Helped the (1,000's)---John 6:9-11
He Helped 70---Luke 10:1
He Discipled the (12)---Luke 6:13-16
He Zeroed in on the (3; Peter, James, John)---Luke 9:28
He Entrusted the Ministry to (1)---John 21:15-19

Again, Jesus loved the whole world. He made Himself available to anyone that would come around. He helped and influenced seventy men. Jesus chose twelve men and He established, equipped and trained them and invested in them to be like Him in order to propagate His mission. He invested all of Himself into three of them, and He invested His time, energy, possessions, privacy, and sanity with all twelve of them all the time, every week, every month, for years. From the disciples' standpoint, they dropped off their professions and abandoned their previous plans for their lives; they denied themselves and their aspirations in life and lived for Jesus and His mission. This was discipleship.

You and I do not live in a perfect world. Subsequently, not all discipleship may follow the precisely same model and pattern that Jesus exemplified. In some cases, there may be partial or temporal disciple making arrangements as per the choice of both parties and depending upon the circumstances at hand. For example, I personally hope to have at the minimum a few years with a man. However, if circumstances allot that I only am given a year or a few months, then I have to accept the circumstances and work with the individual so that we can be good stewards of the time that God permits us together (1 Corinthians 7:24).

Disciple making is deeper and more involved in another person's life. Discipleship transforms disciples into friends. Jesus said in John 15:14-15: *"Ye are my friends, if ye do whatsoever I command you. Henceforth I call you not servants; for the servant knoweth not what his lord doeth: but I have called you friends; for all things that I have heard of my Father I have made known unto you."* When you disciple someone, you allow them to come close into your life and be your friend. In this friendship, just as the Lord Jesus informed us with our friendship with Him, we allow our disciples to understand us and to know what we are doing. This permits a bond and trust to be created. Meanwhile, we allow our disciples to catch the concept of our passions, and the vision of Christ's mission.

On an important side note, even though we might say "our disciples," they really are not our disciples. In all reality, they are Christ's disciples. They belong to Him. He is just permitting us to be a conduit tool to facilitate growth in their lives. Therefore, we need to be careful how we throw these possessive words "our, mine, yours" around, and make sure that we correctly understand that people belong to the Lord, not us. We need to make sure that we reflect all possessiveness back to the Lord Jesus. The Lord Jesus made sure to teach Peter this principle when Jesus told him three times in John 21:15-17 to *"feed my lambs…feed my sheep…*[Peter] *feed my sheep."* Peter learned the lesson well. We know this because years later Peter admonished some church overseers to *"feed the flock of GOD* [emphasis added]" in 1 Peter 5:2. He reminded them that the flock is not their flock, but the flock is God's flock.

The Apostle Paul understood this important truth too. He understood that those whom he served belonged to God and they were preciously dear to the heart of God. This understanding gave his heart room to feel very close to those whom he served. He always had an attitude of calling God's precious dear ones, those whom he served, as his little children and referred himself as being their spiritual father. For example, this is revealed to us in his writings of 1 Corinthians 4:14-16 to those at Corinth when he compared his discipleship relationship with these individuals as being a spiritual father to someone, and then becoming a spiritual grandfather, and eventually then a spiritual great-grandfather and so forth. He took his discipleship relationships to the umpth degree. His relationships were more than just a once a week meeting at a church. His heart embraced people with the outlook as if they were inner family to him.

There are countless men out there who want to instruct others in the Word of God, but who do not desire to personally invest in-depth time of their lives into other's lives. Such men miss out on all the joys and sorrows of literally watching someone over time transform into the person that God intends them to be. Discipleship goes beyond being an instructor or a teacher. Discipleship is taking on that roll of being a spiritual father to someone and taking the responsibility for the overall development of an individual. Disciple making involves being that spiritual father and serving another by getting in the dirty trenches of another's life and working alongside them in their troubles and perhaps sinful garbage. Disciple making involves being by their side in the thickets of the good and bad times of life, even in sin, and guiding them to seek God and to know God, and to become solely dependent on God.

Jesus demonstrated this fatherly servant hood principle in John 13: 4-15 for us, too. In this passage of scripture, in particular to verse 4, it says, "*He* [Jesus] *riseth from supper, and laid aside his garments; and took a towel, and girded himself.*" Here we see at this time that Jesus set His role aside as being their teacher and in place took on the role of being their lowly servant. Then we know the rest of the story—that Jesus got down on his hands and knees and humbly washed His disciples' feet.

Discipleship is not after the big crowd, the mass of Christians. Discipleship is after the few, the one individual needing help. Discipleship is not always a clean and fun vocation. Many times, it is dirty, rough, and sorrowful. Discipleship involves being faithful to people and with patience repeatedly training them on a regular basis (living the Bible out before their eyes). We should never, never give a lot of rules or a list of things to do to a disciple. Christianity is not a bunch of rules or a list of ways to live. If we are going to make God-fearing disciples, we must live out the biblical truths before their eyes. First Timothy 4:12 instructs us that we should be an example of the believers in Word, in conversation, in charity, in spirit, in faith and in purity. We should seldom tell someone what we could demonstrate before him through our actions, according to 1 Peter 5:3. Though discipleship involves teaching, the demonstration of truth through a godly lifestyle should be emphasized more than a verbal teaching of truth. This way, when opportunities of teaching do arise for us disciple makers, our disciples will already have an example to learn from concerning some sort of truth that we are trying to teach them. For, disciple making does involve repeatedly teaching (telling and explaining the truth) an individual to deny sinful actions, habits, and lifestyles and to embrace holiness within the individual's heart and to focus on giving their life to Jesus through the giving of themselves into another individual's life. However, it is much more profound when a disciple has been given a personal demonstration of a biblical truth. For example, I personally always go into the work of discipleship with every man that I work along with a deliberate wise attitude, the attitude that every biblical principle that needs to be instilled into him will have to be repeated at least 1,000 times before he will grab hold of the truth and implement it into his own life. Therefore, patience is extremely essential in discipling a man. If we are filled with genuine love for an individual, such as a father possesses for his child, then we will be enabled to patiently work alongside a man for the long-term benefit of his life.

In discipleship, you first start seeking God in prayer, and ask God to give you a person who has a heart after His so that you can work with him or her. I caution you that God will answer your prayer and He just might give you someone who sincerely desires to know God, but who currently is enwrapped in sin, strongholds, and bad decisions (Mark 2:17). Whoever God gives you, be satisfied with the work, fervent in prayer, and joyful in the baby steps of growth. Men should disciple men or boys, and women should disciple women or girls. You cannot have two or more disciples until you have had one and learn the ropes of the investment from just one. After you learn some of the ropes, God may promote you to disciple more than one at a time. Whichever the case, keep your heart focused on the few or the one. This is where the power of disciple making shines forth from.

The task of a disciple maker is not to teach knowledge to another Christian: it is to establish the young Christian to be dependent on God and equip the young Christian through the truths and obedience of God's Word. Discipling someone involves faithfully teaching and training someone in righteous living (obedience toward God) and the Word of God (dependence on God) on a regular basis. These two ways complement one another. They work hand-in-hand so that a disciple can eventually catch Christ's vision and learn to become fruitful through doing the same by getting involved into someone else's life too. You will teach the person truths from the Bible. This is through instructing from the Word and explaining biblical truths. Meanwhile, you will also train an individual those biblical truths. This involves you exemplifying and modeling biblical truths and living a God-fearing biblical lifestyle in front of the young Christian. One day of example outweighs ten years of teaching. Training can only be done through interaction with someone. This is why I personally like to take men fishing, camping, go run errands with me, go shopping at the grocery store together, or go witnessing together. I want the men I am working with to interact with me in different life situations and experiences and learn to be Christ-like in all circumstances of life.

Discipleship is great because the young Christian is given the opportunity to see realness of a Christian. The disciple maker also is human, so another great thing about discipleship is that the young Christian will have numerous opportunities to see his discipler's strengths and his weaknesses as well; such as his failures, his shortcomings, and needs. I always tell men around me that the more they spend time with me, the more they are going to observe that I have many frailties and that I too need more of God's touch in my life. I do not worry about making a mistake in front of the men I work with, and I recommend that you do not worry either. This will work out for the better in them in the long run. Your disciple needs to know that you are human too and it is beneficial for him to witness that you too have personal struggles and areas to be improved in. Through training, the young Christian will observe what is well to do, what is effective and wise to do, but also he has opportunities to observe what is incorrect to do or what is not effective in helping others.

I personally love discipling young Christians because they are very uncouth with their speech, unlike older, polished Christians. God uses young Christians in my life to correct me sometimes in areas that need to be better. I have experienced many times being reproved by a young Christian over something silly. I never lash back at them for observing my mistakes and correcting me. Instead, I always listen to what they energetically and boldly tell me and I ponder their words. Sometimes they are right and sometimes they are mistaken, but I do listen and consider what God might be trying to teach me through their correction or ignorance.

The Bible teaches that we are to bear much fruit and fruit that remains. In the Holy Bible the word "fruit" does not always denote food, such as apples or bananas. Fruit in the Bible can also denote people, such as in John chapter 15. Here, in John chapter 15, Jesus taught that God is glorified when we bear much fruit and fruit that remains. Getting involved in another individual's life, which means helping them with their problems, and discipling them, is the method that God designed for us to bear MUCH FRUIT THAT REMAINS. God is not just interested in people who receive Him as their Savior and that's all, for He is the One who originates fruit (Hosea 14:8b and John 15:4). If He were solely interested in short-lived fruit—merely believers—then He would have commissioned us just to preach His Gospel. God is interested in long-term results—disciples. For, the Bible emphatically teaches that Jesus came to make disciples and not mere believers on Him (John 8:31, John 13:35, John 15:8, and Acts 14:22). Jesus wants Christians who will follow Him with commitment. The way Christians prove their commitment is to go out and make more disciples and to teach them to fruitfully make more disciples and so forth.

Let's look at a physical example from the passage of John chapter 15. John 15:1-8 uses that word "fruit." Again, the fruit that the Lord is talking about here is not merely in relation to physical fruit such as apples, neither is it in relation to the fruit of the Spirit: love, joy, peace, longsuffering, gentleness, goodness, faith, meekness, and temperance.

The Bible speaks of different types of fruit. Another example, the fruit of the womb, is a woman's baby. The fruit of the Spirit are nine distinctive outcomes or results that are manifested from us as we focus and are connected and influenced by the Spirit of the Lord Jesus. These nine outcomes are the result of the Spirit doing something in and through us as we yield to Him. Another, greater, fruit that John chapter 15 is speaking about is souls. God is interested in us not to just bear inward results through communion with Him, but He is also interested in us having outward results (fruit) in bearing people. For Proverbs 11:30 says, *"The fruit of the righteous is a tree of life."* This terminology of fruit bearing is consistent with New Testament texts, such as John chapter 15, which clearly refer to soulwinning as we practice it.

We see in the first chapter of the Holy Bible that what God has created always brings forth fruit after its own kind. For example, the fruit of an apple tree is not an apple in the end result. The fruit of an apple tree is another apple tree. If you take an apple off the apple tree and plant the apple, you will eventually get another apple tree. Therefore, this tangible example shows us that the fruit (the results) of the righteous believers would be other people becoming righteous. The righteous "turn many to righteousness" and this activity is called a tree of life. Therefore the fruit (results) of the soulwinner is the activity of creating another soulwinner, someone who invests their time, energy and efforts into the lives of others to bring them to Christ and to disciple them to then become disciple makers themselves. Therefore, Matthew 28:19-20's Great Commission's fruit does not call us only to get one saved, but the end fruit of the Great Commission, the end result is to get someone saved, to get him baptized, to get him to have fellowship with God, and also to get him to go make other disciples as himself.

You can mentor someone for a planned few days to years. On the contrary, discipleship takes much more time. Disciple making takes years, maybe even a whole lifetime. It took Jesus three and a half years to make His disciples into the results that He wanted. You cannot disciple someone in one month, or one year. It very rarely takes months and it almost always takes years to get a man on the road to maturity and intimate fellowship with Christ, victorious over the sins and the recurring problems that come along with a young Christian. If you are going to disciple individuals, then you must realize that you must and you need to actively pray for them often, fellowship with them often outside of a church building, and get into the Word of God with them often and as much as possible outside of a church building.

Discipleship means that you are going to spend productive time with an individual outside of a church building and develop a real friendship with someone. Discipleship does not take place inside the church building or even in a classroom setting. It takes place off church grounds and involvement in common life areas, the real world. For example, you may purposefully cut time out of your schedule and meet up with a young Christian every other morning for prayer and Bible devotions for a few months. Young Christians need to learn how to productively spend time with God and be fed from the Bible and how to pray. It is what John the Baptist did with his disciples. He taught them to pray, Luke 11:1. Or, you may agree to hang out with a young Christian once a week at a nearby park and spend some time in the Bible together. Whatever arrangement you make, you must understand that a young Christian does not know how to feed himself from the Word, just as a physical newborn baby does not know how to feed himself. This is why he needs a mature Christian to help feed Him until He learns to grab onto the Bible himself. Discipleship requires us doing work and ministry with new baby Christians. It demands character training and learning life skills mingled with the Bible. It requires spontaneity as well as structure. Training someone's intellect can occur in a classroom or at a church setting, but discipleship can only occur in the context of day-to-day living.

A disciple maker's responsibility is to provide an environment that will enhance the growth process of a disciple. This only happens outside of the church building. You are the human agency that God uses to help him put on and adjust Jesus' yoke, so he can learn to feed from Jesus and grow in maturity (Matthew 11:29). You must not imagine that it is up to you to cause a disciple's growth. That's God's job. You cannot do it. Nor should you think that you are the only one needed to set up an agreeable environment for him. God will use your involvement in his life along with other variables to bring about growth in his walk with the Lord. All you and I are to do in the process, in other words, is become a doormat to that person. A disciple maker will stick with someone when the good times are great and when the bad times come and life gets dirty and difficult.

Physical newborn babies have dirty diapers that need to be changed often. Spiritual newborn babies have dirty diapers too. Consequently, as disciple makers, you and I must be there to long-sufferingly put up with some bad habits sometimes and correct them, and guide them to the cleaning truth. As a personal example, I long-sufferingly worked with a man who at first could not get rid of the bad habit of using a foul mouth. When we were together and when he would curse, I did not adamantly jam down Bible verses into him. Instead, I patiently sometimes ignored his mouth but other times I lovingly referred our conversations to Bible verses that exhort us to speak gracious and useful words that exhort and encourage one another. He, like others, is better able to receive the Word's correction through our human charity (love) than through human rejection and me adamantly always judging and rebuking him. If you disciple someone, there will be times when you just have to patiently put up with their stubborn habits, and there will indeed be times where you will have to lovingly rebuke them from the Word over actions or decisions they make. I personally never enjoy doing the rebuking but it is a responsibility that must be done. The wisdom is to know when to put up with one's bad habits and when to lovingly correct them.

A young Christian must learn how to make right decisions that please God. He must be warned of the various glittery worldly and religious attractions that are likely to reach out with their octopus arms and pull him in and sidetrack him. Paul knew this and this is why he penned down the words: "*But we were gentle among you, even as a nurse cherisheth her children: So being affectionately desirous of you, we were willing to have imparted unto you, not the gospel of God only, but also our own souls, because ye were dear unto us*" in 1 Thessalonians 2:7-8. Whether we are mentoring or discipling someone, we need to make sure that we love on them all the time. May we be gentle with them. May we cherish them through much prayer and a lifestyle of concern for them. If we desire for them to know God then we must be willing to impart not only the Word of God but also our own lives into their lives. They are very dear to Christ, and they should be dear to us, too.

CHAPTER 10

The Objectives of
Discipling and Mentoring

Herein is my Father glorified, that ye bear much fruit;
so shall ye be my disciples.
− John 15:8

There is supposed to be a purpose and goal for mentoring and discipling young Christians. Paul writes in Ephesians 4:11-12: "*And he* [God] *gave some, apostles; and some, prophets; and some, evangelists; and some, pastors and teachers; For the perfecting of the saints, for the work of the ministry, for the edifying of the body of Christ.*" The objective of mentoring and discipling is not to go on endlessly teaching the young Christian so that he is always at the receiving end. The aim is not to make him dependent on the one who is mentoring or discipling him. The goal is to establish and then equip the young Christian with the tools so that he will learn to intimately love and know God (Deuteronomy 6:5) and to learn to take his place along with other believers in building the body of Christ (Joel 1:3); he will eventually learn to be a disciple maker too. He must become a mature Christian dependent on God, mature in love, taking his part in the corporate growth of the body of Christ.

Then Paul continues to explain in Ephesians 4:13-16: "*Till we all come in the unity of the faith, and of the knowledge of the Son of God, unto a perfect man, unto the measure of the stature of the fullness of Christ: that we henceforth be no more children, tossed to and fro, and carried about with every wind of doctrine, by the sleight of men, and cunning craftiness, whereby they lie in wait to deceive; But speaking the truth in love, may grow up into him in all things, which is the head, even*

Christ: From whom the whole body fitly joined together and compacted by that which every joint supplieth, according to the effectual working in the measure of every part, maketh increase of the body unto the edifying of itself in love." These verses tell us a lot of important truths, but the principal point that these verses are conveying is that the young Christian should not over time become a midget in his faith, but grow and become balanced and stable in his faith, not carried away by "*every wind of doctrine.*"

None of this can come about with a disciple maker demanding, "Believe this and that"; that is with force and God never forces anyone to do anything, and neither should we (1 Peter 5:3). Christianity is not by force, but by love. Instead, all of this can come about with the humble insistence that a Christian establish his life with the standards of pleasing Jesus. A disciple maker must impart to a young Christian that they must always keep their life measured by the standards of Jesus, not by the standards of men. I will admit that for most people it takes God some time to get us out of the way of thinking that unless everyone sees as we do, they must be wrong. That is never God's view. The disciple maker must not get impatient. He must remember how long-sufferingly the Lord has personally dealt with him—with great patience and gentleness; but at the same time, the disciple maker must never water down the truth. He must always keep in mind that Jesus commissioned us to go make disciples, "*Teaching them to observe all things whatsoever I have commanded you.*" He did not commission us to make new converts to our opinions or demands. With this in mind, a new convert will have potential to be shaped to know Jesus and to become dependent on Him alone.

There should be a threefold growth which a Christian should look for in those whom he mentors or disciples. First, there must be maturity in love (Ephesians 3:17-19). Second, there must be soundness of doctrine (1 Timothy 4:16). Third, they must be involved in building up the church

(Hebrews 10:24-25 & 1 Thessalonians 5:11); however, not the church organization, but the living body of Christ—people. Christian behavior, Christian belief, and Christian service must go together. Growth must be manifested in all of these three realms. These three realms are the results that prove we are His disciples as Jesus exhorted us to search for in John 15:8, Matthew 7:20, and Matthew 12:33.

Our world is so messed up in its standards and values. We Christians should invest our lives into the lives of new believers so that they can learn that it is a worthy obligation to stand true to the unwavering standards and values of godliness. Their learning of this obligation should not just come from the Word of God, but they should learn through their observations of us living godly lifestyles. It is true that the miracle of the new birth does alter a person's basic attitudes and changes the direction of his life, but the constant teaching and training of the Word of God is necessary to establish a new believer in the Kingdom's way of life. For example, men call out to Jesus and believe on Him for salvation, and they start that relationship with God and are completely unaware of things within themselves that God is not for. God still accepts them as His child, but He does not desire for them to continue to be ignorant of His ways. This is why we need to disciple them and get them into the Holy Bible so that they can learn areas within their own lives that they need to be empowered by the Holy Spirit to change or stop doing, such as evil communications (Ephesians 4:29), disobedience to authorities (Titus 3:1), or unnecessary association with the ungodly (Psalm 1:1). Christian behavior is not to be the consequences of rules and man-inspired traditions. Christian behavior is to be the product of biblical mentorship and discipleship along with a saturation of the Word of God. A young Christian who is growing will gradually learn to adjust his attitudes and conducts so that they will honor and please God. This will be well pleasing in the sight of the Lord.

Many Christians often are caught between the crosscurrents of non-Christian philosophies and ideologies. Most of the other religions in the world are resurgent and have a false sense of spirituality in their appeal. To be a Bible believing disciple of Jesus Christ in today's generation is many times against our culture's norms and values of the present day. Subtle pulls for compromises are increasing more and more. These subtle, ungodly compromises have silenced many Christians from voicing out their witness of the cross of Jesus Christ. The increasing popular numbers of many "spiritual" people are deceiving numerous followers by the millions and are waxing worse and worse, deceiving and being deceived, as is indicated would happen in the last days according to 2 Timothy 3:13. These so-called "spiritual" teachers, such as some of the popular television and internet sensationalists, have much popular appeal to young Christians and definitely to the world. Even more sadly is that these ever-growing "spiritual" people are infiltrating the churches today. Just as was prophesied in 1 Timothy 4:1 many old time nominal Christians are laying down their sound biblical doctrines, values, and the Bible itself and becoming followers of this worldwide demonic teaching of "spiritualism." Their teachings are very subtle, counterfeiting Christian principles and teaching many philosophies and vain deceits that sound good on the surface, but have no basis near the saving Cross of Jesus.

If old-time Christians are being led astray, then how much easier is it for these deceiving "spiritual" leaders to lure in young Christians into their false and seemingly harmless teachings from the Bible and other books? For this reason, God warned us with the admonishment in Colossians 2:8: *"Beware lest any man spoil you through philosophy and vain deceit, after the tradition of men, after the rudiments of the world, and not after Christ."* We are admonished to beware, meaning to be wary, cautious, and to be careful with whom we allow our eyes to see and our ears to listen to. Just a few verses before in Colossians 2:4, he makes mention why we are to beware of such false teachings: "*lest any man should beguile you with enticing words.*" Beguile means to delude, to deceive, or to impose on by artifice or craft; such as, Satan did with Eve in the Garden of Eden. He very cunningly spoke God's Word in such a misrepresented manner that his lies sounded as truth and she was deceived. She believed his cunning lies. Satan is using the same cunning craftiness of lies through all of his false teachers in the world today. They sound fine, but they are not truth. They are lies. This is why we need to guide new believers to become as Colossians 2:7 says, "*Rooted and built up in him* [Jesus], *and* [e]*stablished in the faith, as ye have been taught, abounding therein with thanksgiving.*"

How wonderful God is! God gave us the remedy in how we can beware of these false teachers and how we can be wise. God gave us the beautiful words in the Psalm, chapter one. Psalm 1:1 says, "*Blessed is the man that walketh not in the counsel of the ungodly, nor standeth in the way of sinners, nor sitteth in the seat of the scornful.*" Let's break this down for a moment. God is saying *blessed,* that means that he is happy; he has no hindrances in his relationship with the Lord; there is peace. Then the verse continues to say, "*is the man that walketh not in the counsel of the ungodly.*" To not walk in the counsel of the ungodly is to not take repetitive steps in their erroneous ways. For example, one manner in which a young Christian needs to be taught is to abstain from focusing his attention on preachers on the television and to instead open up his Bible and a Bible Concordance, and to study the Bible himself. Though I am not against all television preachers, I will admit that the overwhelming majority of them are hogwash and garbage. Most appropriately, I like what these hogwash preachers are really referred to as in the Bible—false prophets. Jesus warns us in Matthew 7:15 for us to beware of false prophets who are WOLVES in sheep's clothing, meaning they appear as a Christian but they are full of hogwash and garbage. These are the types of people which Philippians 3:2 warns us about. Philippians 3:2 admonishes us to *"Beware of dogs, beware of evil workers, beware of the concision."* Therefore, I personally like to recommend men around me to do activities that are more profitable for them in the long run, such as opening up a concordance along with their Bible and to study different words or subjects in the Bible. For example, a good word to look up and study is the word "please". Then to read all the verses that contain the word "please" within them. While reading these verses, make a list of all the verses that have to do with God and the word "please". After the study, an individual will have a long list of things that the Lord is pleased with and is not pleased with. This particular activity and many others are a lot more profitable than sitting in front of television preachers.

Let's return to Psalm 1:1. The next section of the verse reads, *"nor standeth in the way of sinners."* To stand in the way of sinners means to hang out and be influenced by their flawed courses of life. A young Christian needs to be warned to guard himself from hanging out with people who will not influence him to know Jesus more and to obey Jesus. This includes staying away from explicit, wicked individuals, but it also includes staying way from people who may eloquently sound good or look good but they never point you to Jesus Christ and Him alone, such as many false preachers on the television or people in our communities. The Bible instructs us in 2 Timothy 3:5 to stay away from individuals who have a form of godliness, but really are not godly at all. Many times when I am spending time with a man I am discipling, I'll ask him questions about who in his life does he think does not encourage him to know God better. If he gives me a response, then I will ask him what he thinks about that. I many times take him to Bible passages such as 2 Timothy 3:1-5 which talk about certain individuals we are not to engage a friendship with. After we read the scriptures, I might ask him if there is something that he thinks he needs to change in his life. I try to avoid telling him who to stay away from. I like to keep room open for the Holy Spirit to direct him and not me. This way he will not become dependent on me, nor will he be able to praise or criticize me in the future over an unforetold event. I only bring up questions to him and point him to the Bible. When he realizes who is not helping him to know God, then he will be able to make a prudent decision and give God the praise for his enlightenment.

Then, in the last section of the Psalm 1:1 verse, it says, *"nor sitteth in the seat of the scornful."* A Christian is not to sit in the seat of the scornful. The scornful are those individuals who avoid truth and are critical and negative to the truths of the Bible. All Christians should not allow themselves to be positioned around wicked people who will influence their thinking in an ungodly manner. For example, we should stay away from those individuals who teach this new age idolatry "spiritualism" that we are strong and need to look deep within ourselves for the power. This is evil. The only Person we should look to for power and assistance is the Lord Jesus Christ. Not ourselves! There is nothing good within ourselves (Romans 7:24). We are not God, nor do we have the power to help ourselves (Matthew 5:3). Only Jesus does! This is why I am always reminding myself and the men around me that like Matthew 6:33 warns us to do, we must daily seek Jesus Christ and Jesus Christ alone. I warn the men around me to stay away from anything that appears to be usurping some glory from Christ and giving it to something or someone else.

These three points should remind mentors and disciple makers to guard themselves as well as to teach their young Christians to be cautious of whom they spend time with and whom they allow themselves to be influenced by. These points should remind us to be very wary of participating in things that draw our attention away from the Cross and lure us closer unto the traditions of the world and "spiritual" people. If the people around us are not repeatedly pointing us to Jesus, then they are probably teaching or living with the rudiments of the world, and not that of Christ. From such people we are to stay away from (2 Timothy 3:5).

Added to all of this is the theological confusion within Christendom. In such a situation, Christian belief must be clearly defined with sound biblical doctrine and established on the offensive and hopeful fundamentals of the Gospel of Jesus Christ in love to the young Christians. The young Christians must learn where to turn in their Bibles for the authority of their faith in Jesus, and they must learn how to submit to that authority at all times.

It is not enough to have godly Christian behavior and be established in the right Christian doctrines. The new believer must also be involved in Christian service as a member of the body of Christ. This is why, as a personal example, I like to do what Elijah did with Elisha in 2 Kings 2. I encourage the men around me to go out and serve people with me. Either through soulwinning activities, or going over to someone's house or place in the city; we go out together and serve people in some capacity. Other times, we get together and serve people through prayer, and sometimes I encourage the men to come with me and do some volunteer work around the church house. All these ways demonstrate to a new believer that they need to give of themselves to others around them. It helps them learn to take the focus off themselves and to look around and serve people all around them.

More importantly, as I serve men around me, I always have in the back of my mind to teach and train them to have a mind for future generations and become servants for these future generations. Psalm 78:4-7 says, "*We will not hide them from their children, shewing to the generation to come the praises of the LORD, and his strength, and his wonderful works that he hath done. For he established a testimony in Jacob, and appointed a law in Israel, which he commanded our fathers, that they should make them known to their children: That the generation to come might know them, even the children which should be born; who should arise and declare them to their children: That they might set their hope in God, and not forget the works of God, but keep his commandments.*" The Bible teaches us that we are not to hide them, that is the truths of God, from our children; not just our physical children, but also our spiritual children. We are to train them up, as Jesus commissioned in Matthew 28:19-20, to extend their horizons, look down the road of life, and serve other younger Christians through discipleship and mentorship. As I serve people around me, I have the outlook to demonstrate before them and to teach them that they should be looking to serve younger Christians than themselves, so that they can help these younger Christians to reproduce themselves for future generations. The key to extending the Kingdom of God is to disciple spiritual children and help them to get a focus to disciple others, who will disciple others, and who will disciple others, and so on. In this way, the Gospel and the investment of lives will continue way into the future even when you and I are long passed on and in Heaven.

I am only one man. I am limited in the number of people I can reach. You and I are limited to the number of people that God can permit us to disciple and invest our lives into. Yet, God gloriously instructs us in Psalm 2:8 to ask Him and He shall give us the uttermost parts of the earth for our possession. That's what the verse says. Go read it. So, did God make a mistake in His promise? I think not! Then how is it possible that God can allow me or you to ask Him for the uttermost parts of the earth, even places that we will never ever go to or see? I'll tell you the answer. The answer is through DISCIPLESHIP!

I, as one man, will never be able to reach every man on this earth. However, if I multiply myself into the lives of others, then other men that I have invested my life into will go beyond me and reach people that I directly cannot reach. So, as a personal example; if in my lifetime or in your lifetime, either one of us has the privilege to thoroughly disciple, let's say, three men, and those three men disciple three men, we will now have nine disciples. If those nine disciples go out and disciple three men, we now have twenty-seven disciples. If those twenty-seven disciples go out and disciple three men, we now have eighty-one disciples. If those eighty-one disciples go out and disciple three men, we now have two-hundred-forty-three disciples, and those two-hundred-forty-three disciples disciple three men, we now have a whopping seventy-hundred-twenty-nine men who are disciples of Christ. As you see, after a few generations, with just using the plausible number three, God will have permitted my or your life to have an impact on countless numbers of people that we will never have gotten to meet.

Or, think about this for another illustration: what would you rather have, a million dollars a day for thirty days or a dollar doubled each day for thirty days? Adding up a million dollars a day for thirty days gives you only $30 million. That sounds like a whole lot. But in comparison, it is only a drop in the bucket to what a dollar multiplied by the factor of two for thirty days gives you: a whopping $536,870,912! There certainly is a tremendous power to multiplication rather than addition. Jesus knew this and this is why He forsook the popular incompetent style of adding disciples (a focus on quantity), and instead went the competent route by investing His life into the lives of the few: twelve men. After Jesus was gone and back in Heaven, these men went out and multiplied themselves, and as a result the multiplicity has continued throughout the generations, and now billions have come to hear the Gospel and call upon Christ as their Savior.

In the few churches today where there is consistent teaching of sound scripture, most believers are faithful in their witnessing and in their service. Sometimes, Christians withhold the whole counsel of God, fearing lest they lay unnecessary burdens on new believers. But, let us not forget the commission of our Lord Jesus, "*teaching them to observe ALL things*" that He has commanded us. Therefore, we are to teach all the counsels of God and lay not down any of His counsel. For example, even after many years of their existence, there are still many churches that are not financially self-supporting. The reason is that the believers in the early days of their congregations had not been taught to give according to the biblical pattern. In the same way, missionary vision and concern is very much lacking in many churches. The biblical understanding of missions has not been given to the believers and they are not aware of their responsibility in world evangelization. These vital failures, as examples, in the mentoring and disciple making of the early new converts and young Christians has led to years and years of stagnant, powerless Christianity throughout the world. For such reasons, new converts and young Christians must be taken under the wings of a Christian who not only knows about God, but who <u>knows God</u> and to be taught and trained through mentorship or discipleship in Word, prayer, and livelihood on a regular basis. We must always be ready (Romans 1:15) to serve our men around us whether if we feel like it or not (2 Timothy 4:2) and we must *teach them to observe ALL* things that Jesus has commanded us in Matthew 28:20.

Last, we soulwinners need to remember the precious instructions found in 2 Timothy 3:14: *"But continue thou in the things which thou hast learned and hast been assured of, knowing of whom thou hast learned them."* We need to daily continue in the truths of the Word and be diligent in the Great Commission of our Lord Jesus Christ in the lives of others. This is wise and worthy unto the Lord Jesus for us to do.

CHAPTER 11
Start Investing Your Life into Someone Today

And I will very gladly spend and be spent for you;
though the more abundantly I love you, the less I be loved.
– 2 Corinthians 12:15

The question now is, "How to disciple or mentor young Christians so as to meet the needs that I have just brought before you and how to fulfill the goals that have been laid down in the previous chapters?" If you ask Christians today these two questions, the big majority would respond with an answer pointing all the work to the man preaching from the pulpit—the pastor. Oh, how sad that is. It is very sad that so many Christians think that all of God's work is designed for the preacher, the pastor! How even more sad to find that there are many pastors and preachers out there who ignorantly believe this and place an unbearable amount of work on themselves. What a heavy burden! What an impossible and difficult burden as well! Think about this. One pastor for 50, 100, or even more people is a very difficult and an impossible responsibility in the training of people to effectively accomplish the Great Commission. This ratio is wrong and unbearable. God understood that such a ratio would kill His work. Therefore, when God originally planned how big the "Christian classroom" should be, He designed the perfect model, as explained in the book of Numbers, and He assigned one tribe, the Levites, to minister to twelve tribes of Israel. Thus, God designed the perfect model: the 1/12 ratio. Then when Jesus came on the scene in this earth, He too understood that the burden of trying to help mass groups of people would be so heavy and impossible to accomplish that Jesus, the Master Planner, refused to engage in such insanity. Instead, Christ exemplified sense by selecting and discipling the few. Ministry leaders, disciple makers, and mentors much look beyond the size of the group of people they have, and within their group of people, no matter what size it is, they merely must and have to select a few faithful candidates, as Jesus did (Luke 6:12-13) whom they will invest their lives into. Or alternatively, the propagation of the Kingdom of God will die.

It is no wonder why the average time for a pastor to stay with a church is three years or less. Many are quitting the vocation and returning to secular occupations. And if pastors are quitting, then just think about all the unlearned believers out there. What are they going to do? For these insane reasons did Jesus model discipleship for us so that we could see that the pastor, the preacher, nor any Christian can invest all of his time, energy, and resources into every single individual around them. For the Christian who believes that all the work is the duty of the pastor or the preacher, their belief is insane. Yes, the pastors and preachers have an important role in God's work, but so does every other Christian. The work of the pastors and preachers along with some usage of other methods can systematically and collaboratively be productive in disciple making and mentoring young Christians.

In the listing of the various gifts for the building up of the church in Ephesians 4:11, Paul does join the duties of the pastor and the teacher together. The pastoral ministry and teaching ministry are two sides of the same coin. The pastor is also the principal teacher of a local congregation of believers. No faithful shepherd of his flock can abdicate his responsibility to feed new, young, and mature Christians. It is a great privilege to stand service after service before a congregation and to teach them the riches of God's Word in guiding them along to know Him and to serve Him and the people around us effectively. What a wonderful calling from God! There is no substitute for this! This task must have the top priority in the ministry of a pastor.

Such a systematic teaching of his congregation from the pulpit will demand the best of his gifts, abilities, time, and effort. He who is willing to invest these freely will reap his reward with great joy. The sermons must be planned so that there is order and continuity. His sermons must always be a reminder to his congregation for them to go out and disciple someone and to invest their lives, time, and efforts into the lives of other people. Ephesians 4:12 instructs pastors to use their positions to equip the Christians to go out of the church building and do the work of the ministry, and for the edifying of the body of Christ. What do you think is the work of ministry for Christians? If you guessed the Great Commission, Matthew 28:19-20, then you are correct. What work do you think edifies Christians? If you guessed again the Great Commission, you are right again. Christ's Great Commission for all Christians is the work of ministry they are to do which will edify all believers.

It is the pastor's job to help make sure that his congregation knows why and how to get involved into the lives of other people. It is the pastor's job to demonstrate discipleship, to cheer the congregants to disciple others, and to demonstrate teaching as well as a life that gets involved in people's lives around him. The pastor's teachings must be biblical, practical, and relevant to disciple making. As far as possible, the pastor must occupy his own pulpit every service. Informal discussion times can be planned in other time slots to clarify or discuss the issue raised by the sermon. The pastor must himself live a life involved with disciple making. If he is not doing it, then most likely no one else in the church will invest time and efforts into other person's lives. A pastor of a local church should choose one or a small group of loyal men, and get deeply involved into their lives and train them to do as he is doing within their lives. Then as they start reaching out and discipling others he can continue to act as their "spiritual father figure" through discipleship but as a "grandfather figure" he can teach and train them in how they can be wise disciple makers in the lives of others too. After a few years, many people in the church will start picking up the lifestyle of disciple making and will involve their lives in some form of mentoring or disciple making with other individuals. The pastor who chooses to apply this biblical principle and minister to a core of spiritually qualified men and women will find after a few years that these individuals can begin carrying some of the burden of the church and they can carry on some of the ministry. This pastor will find that his workload will lessen and his time will open up so that he has more time to study and more time to be more effectively and efficiently involved in people's lives.

As I already mentioned, the pulpit ministry needs to be involved with other methods as well. Weekly adult Bible classes also can be useful for systematic teaching. Though I am not one to stress Bible classes, I do find them to be helpful in the growth of Christians. However, I must emphasize that teaching or attending a Bible class should never be defined as discipleship or mentorship.

Just because we get someone to read a piece of knowledgeable information, look up some Bible verses, and write answers to some questions, that does not necessarily mean the individual is gaining any spiritual maturity. We need to be more concerned with the quality and the growth of our disciples rather than the quantity of knowledge they learn. The growing process of disciples involves them "learning" (gaining the information), "loving it" (gaining the conviction), and "living it" (manifesting the information and the conviction in their lifestyles). As disciple makers, we have to pursue that process, not the material-completion process. Disciples are not projects. They are our friends who we should be well concerned for their spiritual maturity.

It would be relatively easy for disciple makers to take important subjects of the Bible for our growing Christians to learn about, and make a nice Bible study series that we could just handout to our disciples and let them go at that. But, that is the criminal way and therefore we do not do that, for two reasons: (1) There are already hundreds, if not thousands, of wonderful Bible studies already available, and (2) We should want to help a disciple become a disciple maker too, not a Bible-study-distributor. There is a big difference between the two. In order for them to learn to become a disciple maker, they must see it lived out before them. That means it is required of us to discern the unique needs of each growing disciple and individually construct a unique program to meet those needs. It requires that we be able to be flexible with the variables of each disciple's life. It requires that we be there to answer the questions that are not in the books. It requires that we be able to bind up the wounds they suffer, and to challenge them to go beyond where they would normally go. The Bible-study-distributor knows nothing of these matters, and his disciples turn out to be mechanical, shallow clones.

This is why we should not prioritize a materials-oriented disciple making program over actual training and teaching the Word with a disciple. I did not say we should not use prepared materials. On the contrary. The wisdom is to know what right materials to use at the right time. I agree with how author Christopher Adsit puts it in his book, *Personal Disciplemaking: A Step-by-step Guide for Leading a Christian From New Birth to Maturity* on pages 99, and 109-110. He says, "the prevalent programs these days employ the shotgun approach: *Fire away—if we leave a big enough crater, we're bound to have hit the target.*" How correct he is. Christians today just want to fill new converts with a bunch of broad knowledge rather than teaching new converts practical truths which can assist them in sensible areas of their lives.

Instead, like Christopher Adsit, I advocate the sharpshooter approach: *Take a good look at the target and then aim at the bulls eye.* Find out what their need is, and apply those studies into a disciple's life.

Today, in most prepared Bible study series, Christians might be doing a real good job teaching disciples important subjects, such as the importance of Christian fellowship (because it's on the schedule), but the next, most crucial step of growth in the disciple's life (and the area in which the Holy Spirit is working) might be in the area of forgiveness. Though the subject of Christian fellowship is important, it is not expedient at the time being for the disciple to learn it. It would be much more desirable for disciple makers to cooperate with God in His program, figure out what the disciple's area of need is, and then use materials designed to meet it. This is much more beneficial for disciples rather than using a scheduled checklist of subjects to guide your teaching lessons.

There are some Christians, as an example, who then might argue, "Hey, a baby Christian needs everything! What difference does it make if you start him with the subject of fasting or witnessing?" I would respond that in the early stages of growth, it may not make much difference… then again, it may make a lot of difference. We do not know. However, we do know that it depends on the individual person, his background, and what GOD WANTS DONE. This is why it is important that we, at all times, show deference to the Holy Spirit's entitlement to decide how a person should be taught. On the other hand, a Bible class or study includes a group of people. Each person is on a different pace and the Holy Spirit is working in different needs of the individuals. This is why we should still give emphasis to what subject should be taught in a small group study, relevant to all disciples, and then it is a good idea to get accustomed to addressing even the new Christian's needs on an individual basis outside of the group Bible study.

I repeat with emphasis that teaching or attending a Bible class should never be defined as discipleship or mentorship. Disciple making and mentoring only can happen outside of a classroom setting and only can occur in a real life setting. They can be used as one of many tools to bring about some clarification to good topics of study and discussion. Bible classes should be designed with the purpose to educate Christians in useful sound biblical doctrines that they can apply to their lives.

The one doing the teaching should go into every Bible study or class with two approaches. First, the teacher should enter every class with the approach that he is going to teach important discipleship principles, but also that he is going to train those discipleship principles into one or a few good men outside the classroom setting. If he does not train (meaning to personally exemplify a lifestyle of disciple making) what he teaches then he is setting up his students to fail in the vocation of disciple making. Secondly, the teacher should have an Ephesians 4:12 attitude to accomplish three goals: (1) To establish the basic truths in Christian lives, (2) To equip the Christians for ministry, and (3) To observe the students, for a purpose to identify and select the one or two students who are good candidates to be discipled. A teacher will be able to recognize who these prospective disciples are because they are very attentive in the classroom by listening and homing in on the teaching; Or, who during or after class ask significant amount of questions which relate to the subject at hand. These good candidates usually come to class ready for the study and they come prepared with their Bible, pen, and perhaps even a notepad. These one or two prospects are then the individuals that the teacher will want to meet up with after class or later during the week and spend extra time with and begin some extra mentoring or disciple making.

Bible study classes can be held in the church building or at someone's home. Preferably at someone's home though. Younger adults can be in one group and the older ones in another group so that there is more freedom in talking and discussion. These groups should not be very large. Interaction and give-and-take in personal relationships are important in this teaching situation. New converts and young Christians feel neglected in the impersonal atmosphere of a church setting. So, it is necessary that they get the care and personal attention they need in these small groups.

These Bible study groups must be informal. Open, frank discussions must be encouraged. Any honest question must be allowed, and the answer found in the group must of course always be directed to the Bible. There must be intimate, transparent fellowship between the one who teaches and those who are taught. Not all the teaching is done by words alone. The responses and the reactions of the one who is the teacher to various situations make a deep impression on new believers. The teacher must be willing to expose himself and his responses to the scrutiny of those who he is teaching in the classroom and discipling outside of the classroom. The teacher must be transparent and real with those whom he teaches and disciples. Disciple making cannot be done from a distance. If we build a wall around ourselves, we cannot make disciples. We must be real with people. For example, a disciple maker (the teacher in this instance) would be wise in the beginning of a relationship with his disciple to gradually increase his transparency with someone. At first, being transparent with a disciple may take the form of sharing with a disciple some of the things a disciple maker has experienced in his fellowship with the Lord. Or, it may involve sharing some of the disciple maker's victories and defeats, successes, and struggles, such as in scripture memory. Little things like that. Then as the relationship grows stronger and the disciple maker and the disciple become more involved in the lives of each other, then the disciple maker can be able to share deeper things, such as the temptations he faces, how he handles them, and his personal battles with the world, the flesh, and the devil.

Such transparency will demonstrate to the disciple that there is a real two-way relationship between the two of you, and he will be more comfortable to learn from you. Remember that a genuine discipleship relationship soon becomes two-way. Your disciple is definitely going to learn a lot from you, but you can learn a lot from him as well. You should eventually let him know that. It would be beneficial for him to genuinely hear you tell him that you need someone like him to keep you accountable, to pray for you, to encourage you, and to teach you. He will be amazed, but through such humility, he will come to understand that we too are just dust of the earth. He needs to know that. By doing this, we not only become true friends with our disciples, but we also help our disciples to eventually get the idea that they need to shift their focus from us and onto Jesus. If we do not accomplish that main point in their lives, then we have made the most serious mistake, idolatry.

There is a costly self-giving of oneself in disciple making. Paul knew this and therefore he wrote in 1 Thessalonians 2:8: *"So being affectionately desirous of you, we were willing to have imparted unto you, not the gospel of God only, but also our own souls* (lives)." Writing to the new believers in the city of Corinth, he said in 2 Corinthians 12:15: *"I will very gladly spend and be spent for you."* As we are well aware of he sure spent himself in the lives of individuals so that they would come into a wonderful fellowship with the Lord Jesus. He was very transparent with them. Therefore, we learn that it is difficult, if not impossible, to be effective in the lives of men unless we are transparent with them. Excellent disciples emerge from the life and the ministry of a transparent disciple maker. Therefore, the question to you is now, "Will you spend and be spent for the souls of other individuals?"

There are two other situations besides the church where mentoring and disciple making should take place. Keep in mind that mentoring and disciple making cannot take place in the church building. It will never happen. Normal life consists outside of the church building and mentoring and disciple making is pertinent to the normalcy of life in learning to be dependent on God. Small Bible study groups in homes can be greatly used to mentor and part of discipling new believers in Word and doctrine. The advantage of this is that the whole family or friends can sit together with the Word of God and study it. This is bound to affect their life in the home and their relationships. Several families in an area can join together and meet regularly to study the Word of God. Such home Bible study groups should be linked with the local church. The local church can provide trained laymen and women to lead these groups. Home Bible study groups are often recommended as very effective means of evangelism. They can also be used for effective mentoring and part of discipling new believers in accordance to principles of sound biblical doctrines.

As I have noted, all Christians, ranging from the pastor to the layman have the high calling of getting involved in the lives of other individuals and to disciple and mentor them. Whatever title we wear in life, we need to get involved in someone's life. We need to pray to God to help us find someone to invest our life into. Then, as we are with these individuals, we need to teach them from the Bible, pray with them, and train them through modeling a biblical lifestyle.

I know of a wise elderly man, Cecil Bean, who, he and his wife have given their lives to the discipling of men and women for approximately fifty years in the ministry. I once heard him state something profound, which over the years I have learned through experience to be true. So we do not get discouraged in the work of God, it is expedient to understand that for every 10 persons asked out to a Bible Study, 1 shows up. For every 10 persons that show up, 1 person becomes a Christian. For every 10 persons that become a Christian, 1 person stays with it. For every 10 persons that stay with it, 1 commits to growing. For every 10 persons that commit to growing, 1 becomes a disciple. For every 10 disciples, 1 becomes a laborer. For every 10 persons that begin to labor, 1 becomes an overseer.

As you go out to labor amongst the people in the world and amongst God's own people, remember those ratios. Hopefully, then you will not become discouraged, nor grow weary or faint in doing good but keep your eyes fixated on Christ. This knowledge and understanding has greatly assisted me to keep persevering when I have felt discouraged and wondered where the results are. God's results take time, and we are given the asset of time to diligently invest our lives into the few that want to grow in the truths of the Lord.

CHAPTER 12

Teach and Train the Basics of what a Young Christian Needs to Know

And how I kept back nothing that was profitable unto you, but have shewed you, and have taught you publickly, and from house to house, Testifying both to the Jews, and also to the Greeks, repentance toward God, and faith toward our Lord Jesus Christ.
— Acts 20:20-21

Jesus said, "*Say not ye, There are yet four months, and then cometh harvest? behold, I say unto you, Lift up your eyes, and look on the fields; for they are white already to harvest.*" Jesus is speaking to His disciples here in John 4:35. He gives an analogy of people compared to grain in a harvest field; specifically the Lord's harvest field of the earth. Jesus told His disciples, that in the Lord's harvest field the grain is plenteous and white to harvest. If we would lift up our eyes and look all around us, we would notice that there are people all around us who are ready to hear the Gospel and be reaped for God.

Then Jesus another time said unto his disciples, "*The harvest truly is plenteous, but the labourers are few.*" Once again, Jesus was speaking to his disciples, this time in Matthew 9:37. He informed them, as well as to us today, that though the harvest of souls is ready to be reaped for God, though many desire to be correctly guided to God, and though there is a great quantity of people who need to hear; the sad truth is that there are few truly qualified laborers to do it. There are a plentiful number of people on this planet who need to be guided to Jesus. There is more work to go around and keep us busy for the rest of our lives.

However, there simply are not a sufficient number of Christians who will rise up and labor for God.

However, I did not bring up these two verses before you to bring your attention about winning the lost to salvation. There certainly is a lack of qualified laborers in the work of proclamation of the Gospel. That glorious work too has insufficient laborers. Nonetheless, there is a worse problem. The work I am referring to is the work of discipling and mentoring new babes in Christ. Not only are there not enough laborers to rise up and preach the Gospel, there are far too few laborers to rise up and invest their lives into the lives of young Christians. This is why Jesus shared with His disciples to look around themselves and see the great needy work of soulwinning. Soulwinning involves not only proclaiming the Gospel and winning someone to Jesus but also investing our lives to be an influence and an impact in other's lives for their need to know and obey God. There just are not enough Christians to do this job. This is why we need to always be begging God to raise up more Christians who will join in the work of this awesome vocation.

If we take our time to invest our lives into people, we can assist in training and teaching young Christians to become one of the few laborers who do choose to rise up and live a life of soulwinning. For this reason, young Christians should be trained and taught as early as possible about the joys of working with Jesus in proclaiming the Gospel and further works of discipleship.

The fact is that most Christians will never become a pastor, evangelist or a clergyman. It is not humanly possible nor is it the will of God for all Christians to work in the clergy. We know this for the simple facts that Ephesians 4:11-12 tell us, and secondly, the renowned "Hall of Faith" in Hebrews chapter 11 makes up of numerous individuals, all of whom were laymen, except for one—Samuel—he was a full time clergyman. It seems that God demonstrates an emphasis on the laymen rather than the clergy. Whichever the case, both are equally important in God's eyes (Acts 10:34).

Though most Christians are not called to be a pastor or an evangelist, the Christian laymen of our local churches do have an equally important part in discipling and mentoring young Christians just as any clergyman does. For example, just as the pastor is an overseer of a local group of believers, each Christian layman can be an overseer in the life of a young Christian; seeing over that the young Christian is taught and trained in the Word, love, and service with God, meanwhile always pointing him to Jesus, while the both of them continue to be part of a local congregation. Yes, we as overseers should always encourage our young Christians to stay in church and learn from the teachings of our pastors and the Word. Nevertheless, most of life occurs outside of the church building. Most of our lives are spent in the community, at the workforce, and in our homes. This is why we need to get involved in people's lives outside of the church building. People live outside of the church building. For another reason, we can be an overseer in people's lives outside of the local church. For example, Christian laymen can mentor or disciple new believers at their place of business. A Christian in industry or in business will have several people working with him. Though the Christian is at that jobsite for a business objective, that business place becomes his sphere of influence for disciple making, or in other words, soulwinning. Not only are his words important, but even his attitudes, his reactions, and his actions speak aloud to those all around him.

One of my friends after work meets up with some of his colleagues in a break room for a small group Bible study. Once a week he teaches them biblical truths and he challenges them from the Bible to get involved in other people's lives too. It has been a wonderful opportunity for my friend as he has seen his colleagues grow in the Lord at his work place. While he is working and getting paid to accomplish his job duties, he lives out the life of Christ before his colleagues (training) and sometimes has the opportunities to speak biblical principles to his colleagues (teaching).

If you work at a business, you too have the same opportunity to lead men and women into the faith and then to build them up in the faith, even while being paid! When a new believer sees discipleship demonstrated right before him in the factory or in the office, the impact is strong. Moreover, this impact does not come from the pulpit or from a paid church staff member, but from one who is like himself in industry or in business to earn his living.

A soulwinner with a passion to obey the Lord's Great Commission may make disciples in a few years among his pupils and his fellow-teachers. A believer who is a layman such as a factory worker or an office worker may do the same among his colleagues. As the discipleship happens within the mundane tasks of life in the community, these believers meanwhile are to be linked to the local church so that they can grow together with the rest of the body of Christ.

The soulwinner who takes on the responsibility to disciple or mentor another believer should work to lead young Christians into seeing the importance of basic biblical truths. The one who is doing the disciple making should live out what he teaches. This is training. For example, anything I teach from the Bible to men around me, I make sure to exemplify through my actions. If I want a young Christian to learn how to witness to people among any setting, like the Bible commands us to do, then I take him along with me in my normal everyday life activities, and sometimes I demonstrate before his eyes how to purposefully witness to strangers while at the grocery store, at the gas station, or even in the library. This way he has not just heard from my mouth that we need to witness all the time, but he is given opportunities to observe and see some ways in how to implement this teaching into practical everyday life situations. Again, we teach from the Bible but we train by our actions. People better retain what they learn through observation and experience with another, than through being taught from a book or a lesson plan.

Another basic biblical truth that we need to help young Christians to understand is to see the importance of the first commandment found in Matthew 22:37; which is to love God with all our heart (our will), all our soul (our emotions), all our mind (our thoughts), and all our strength (our actions). They should be trained and taught from the Bible that the way we deepen our love for God is through personally spending time alone with Him in His Word and prayer. Matthew 6:33 is an excellent verse to teach this important truth that Jesus should be our first priority and focus in everything we do. Every single day, all the time, I remind and encourage Christians around me to be in their Bible. I take normal daily activities and relate them as examples for why we are to be in the Bible with God. Our main objective with young Christians is to train and teach them to become dependent on God and the Word. Why? Because our responsibility is not to make sure that our disciples turn out well. We are not even responsible to make sure they become God-fearing individuals. No, that's God's job. Our job is to point them, direct them, and guide them to God and His Word. And praise the Lord, this sure is comforting to know while doing the work of discipleship. Remember, it is not our teaching that will change lives, but it is the Holy Spirit's conviction from the Word of God that will change lives. If we can get young Christians to understand the importance of being in the Bible and clearly more important to get them to have a lifestyle of being in the Word, then God will be able to transform them into the image of His Son and accomplish His will in and through them (Romans 12:1-2).

Next, young Christians need to learn how to live the second commandment, which is found in Matthew 22:39; that we are to love our neighbors as ourselves. We are to teach them that as they have and make opportunities, they are to do good to all people, but especially to those of the household of faith, as Galatians 6:10 and 1 Peter 2:17

instruct us to do. They need to get involved in other's lives, and to exhort other Christians daily (Hebrews 3:13; Jude 1:3) unto good works (Titus 2:14; 3:8, 14; Hebrews 10:24). Young Christians need to learn through example and teaching that as they gradually grow they need to step out and get involved in someone else's life, too. This is why I call men out around me to go do a specific activity of serving someone with me, such as some type of a soulwinning activity or participate in a Bible study. For example, when I discern that a man is ready, or at least capable of trying, I will call him to go gather some Christians together and lead a little Bible study group with him. Then afterwards, I will follow-up with him and discuss important points with him about what he learned, his concerns, his failures and successes in leading a Bible study group.

A baby Christian, as well as any Christian, will become unsatisfied with his Christianity with just consumption of the Word. If he does not go out and involve and give himself into the lives of others, and pour out of him what God is pouring into him, he will become dissatisfied with his faith. This is true and can be explained through a physical explanation that God has given us on this planet. There are two large lakes in Israel for all Christians to observe and learn an important lesson from: the Sea of Galilee and the Dead Sea. These two Seas can represent the two types of Christians that exist: a Sea of Galilee Christian or a Dead Sea Christian. Both of these Seas have rivers flowing into them, and are both fed by the Jordan River. Though they both are fed the same water from the Jordan River, yet only one Sea possesses life and the other is dead. The Sea of Galilee is a fruitful, healthy lake, full of aquatic life, while the Dead Sea is non-fruitful and void of life. The difference is the outflows of water. The Sea of Galilee has water flowing out of it while the Dead Sea does not have any outlets of water to flow out of it. Because of this, the mineral content in the Dead Sea of the water is extremely high, and therefore chokes out all possibility of life.

This geographical illustration demonstrates how a Christian will be either a fruitful, satisfied Christian or an unfruitful, dissatisfied Christian. The fruitful, satisfied Christian beams with life and is a productive, "healthy" Christian. The non-fruitful, unsatisfied Christian is virtually a dead, "unhealthy" Christian like the Dead Sea. How is this so? It is probably safe to say that like most Christians, the Sea of Galilee and the Dead Sea have inputs. Both Seas have several inputs or waterways that "feed" into them; as well as both of them have the common major water source that feeds into them, the Jordan River. This is good and it is healthy like in the two types of Christians. Like the Seas, Christians have inputs of God feeding them His Word through daily reading and meditation of the Bible, preaching from church, Bible studies, television preaching, radio worship, CD's, DVD's, and so on. Naturally, the "healthy" Christian has more input, so they are typically healthier. However, the bigger difference and the most important to the health of the two Seas and the two types of Christians is the output. The Sea of Galilee has a "healthy" outflow resulting in the Sea teaming with life of all sorts. The Dead Sea has an "unhealthy" virtually no outflow resulting in the Dead Sea being just that, dead! Nothing grows due to the heavy salt content that just sits there. You can literally float on the top of the water. Everything dies in it because there is no outflow. For a Christian to stay as a Sea of Galilee Christian, he must have outflow from his life. He must give of himself of what God has put into him: some examples are by the giving of oneself through soulwinning, serving people, ministering to people, mentoring others, teaching others, or discipling others. If a Christian does not give out what God has put into him, then the Christian's inflow will soon be dry, meaningless, non-productive, and stagnant resulting like the Dead Sea.

We must keep in mind that both Seas have input or an inflow of nourishment and nutrients, but only one of the Seas, the Sea of Galilee, permits these nourishments and nutrients not to just stay in, but to flow through it and back out of it again. This is the one that is healthy and filled with an abundance of all kinds of life. We must choose to be a Christian that resembles the Sea of Galilee; a constant outflow of ourselves to others. We must demonstrate a life of giving before the one's we disciple, and to teach and train them to not only just consume the Word of God but to give it back out of them and outflow it through service into the lives of others. We need to teach and train them that unlike many Christians, if they want to be satisfied with their relationship with God, they must not just take, take, take, but they must also give, give, give. The work of discipleship and teaching and training them to give themselves to others is not just for our health alone, but it is also for a joyous benefit for those we disciple. Therefore, we must get involved in people's lives, and train and teach young Christians to not only daily spend time alone with God in prayer and the Word, to not only go to church as much as possible, but to also learn to get involved in someone else's life around them.

CHAPTER 13

The Responsibility Is Yours

Also I heard the voice of the Lord, saying, Whom
shall I send, and who will go for us?
Then said I, Here am I; send me.
– Isaiah 6:8

The best place for discipling and mentoring young Christians is within the local body of believers, but outside the church building. It is often thought in modern times that if a new believer just attends and sits in every church service where the Bible is taught, he will become strong in the faith and grow in his Christian life. This is a mistaken belief. The church service is supposed to be designed to stimulate Christians to leave the building and spend time alone with God meditating on the particular topic brought up and then to implement (do; put into action) its truths and principles. I certainly am not against church services, but they just are not the place for believers to participate for expediential growth in their relationship with Jesus Christ. The relationship with Jesus Christ does not grow by sitting and listening to what God has taught someone else. The relationship with Jesus Christ grows deeper through spending time alone with Him, and through experiencing His work with other believers in activities such as fellowship, Bible studies, prayer, soulwinning, serving others, and in life general.

There have been many young Christian men and women who have been taught to just come to church faithfully and do nothing else, and these same men and women have ended up as miserable failures in their Christian lives. They have been made much of and regarded as a showcase sample because they wear "appropriate" suits and dresses or because they sit faithfully every single service in the front pew of the church or they smile and shake everyone's hand with a gentle, calm voice. Then very soon, they have become the favorite of many folks and instead of learning to walk in the Light, they fall prey to secret deceptions, sins, and pride in their personal lives.

Unfortunately, too, many new and mature Christians today are stuck in the routine of just going to church and having church services. This is not helping! They are mistakenly cultivating their hearts to a spiritual death and a useless life. We are not commissioned to just attend church services. We are commissioned to be concerned for people and get involved into other's lives or else we will be caught up in that old miserable religion—self. People need help and we are called to help!

In Mark 2:1-12 we see a story where Jesus was inside of someone's house doing some teaching. The house was jammed full with people, so much that there was no way possible to enter the house by conventional ways, such as the doors or even windows. Meanwhile, some friends were very concerned about their friend, who lay with palsy. They had faith in Jesus and they knew that if they could bring their sick friend before Jesus that Jesus would heal their friend. They tried to enter the house through the door and windows, but it was impossible. These friends' faith in Jesus was so confident in Him that they arose to the occasion to help their friend through unconventional, but radical and extreme means. They climbed to the top of the house and lifted their friend onto the roof with them. Then they literally went to the extreme efforts of breaking apart some of the roof, and then they did the unconventional thing; they let down their sick friend into the house before Jesus.

Because of their faith in Jesus, because of their extreme concerns and love for their friend, they chose to use the unconventional methods in order to bring their friend close to Jesus. I am sure that while they were tearing that roof apart that there were people on the ground and inside the building staring at them, and pointing at them, and yelling at them, "Hey, stop that. You are being a nuisance.... Look what you are doing here! Stop!" Nevertheless, they persisted and achieved to bring their friend before Jesus. As a result, their friend was healed, and the Gospel of forgiveness was preached to all that was in attendance that day.

I tell you this story for the simple fact that if we are going to take on the responsibility of disciple making and mentoring young Christians, we have to sometimes take great strides and use unconventional methods of helping people. We have to sometimes go the extreme with love and great concern for people and get into the trenches of individual lives and get down and dirty with them in the mud sometimes. Meaning we have to get down to their lingo (1 Corinthians 14:9), their mind-set, and talk with them the language they understand while giving them the wise Word of God which will lubricate their old sores. I do not mean that we join them in their unproductive self-seeking habits or sins, but that we humble ourselves into a realm of schemes that they understand with conduct and communications in godliness and the Word. If we humble ourselves and get down to their level of understanding and then begin to continue to give more of the Word to them at their need, then the Word will not only lubricate their sores, but the Word of God will begin to bring their sores to an itch, and they will soon say, "Glory! I sure don't need this or that in my life any longer," or "Man! I need to do this or that of what I see from the Word." For example, I know of a man who had the privilege to lead another man to the saving arms of Jesus Christ inside his home. The day the new convert called upon Jesus for salvation he knew very little about the Bible, nor had he ever been accustomed to attend church services. Though the mature Christian encouraged the new convert to come to church with him, it did not click in the new convert's head that he ought to do so. Instead of the mature Christian pushing his conviction onto him that he should attend church services, he patiently met with the new convert on a weekly basis conducting Bible studies with him inside his home. Over an extended period of time the mature Christian faithfully kept feeding him the Word of God and little by little he witnessed the new convert grow in understanding of biblical principles and truths. Much time later, it occurred to the new convert that he ought to make opportunities in his life to be around other Christians. On his own initiative, he eventually decided to start attending church services faithfully.

The moral of the story is that the mature Christian could have chosen to push his convictions upon the new convert and insisted that he go to church, but that would have left the new convert with a bitter taste of Christianity and an abandonment of his new faith. On the other hand, the mature Christian correctly met the new convert where he was in his understanding; a new saved sinner who knew nothing in godly instructions; and the mature Christian patiently loved on him and got into the Bible with him, and he stayed out of the way and allowed God to convince the new convert of truths, specifically the importance to attend church faithfully. The mature Christian fed the new convert the Word and at the same time taught him how to be fed by God and do what God says and not what man says. As a result, today, the new convert attends church and is serving the Lord in wonderful ways.

If we patiently meet people where they are in their understanding of God's truths, and feed them the Word of God over and over, then you and I will see God's transformation in their thinking, then in their decisions and actions, then eventually into their habits, and finally God will begin to teach them to live a holier, godly lifestyle. So too many, new, young, and even older Christians today are stuck in the routine of just going to church and having church services. This is not helping! New, young, and older believers walking with the Lord Jesus need more than church services. We all need that interaction with other believers on a weekly, if not a daily schedule. If Christians are not getting together outside of the church house, then they too will fall prey to the deceptions, sins, and pride of life. For this reason, we need to invite people over to our homes and have fellowship with them. Or, we can meet up with people at parks, libraries, sporting events, at waterfronts, shopping centers, or coffee shops. Only meeting people at the church house is neither practical, nor personal, nor helpful. Spending time with other Christians outside of the church house is practical and it is very personal and helpful. It allows us to be real with each other, and to know each other in deeper ways through experiences and exposures to different environments and events. Jesus not only took his disciples to the synagogues, but also always brought them along with Him for exposure to all types of environments. He would take his disciples to celebrations, people's homes, fishing, boat riding, community events, and funerals. He wanted them to get real Christianity at its best, which only can be seen in the events of life. We need to do the same. How else can we train them?

Another principle that we should understand is that it is also wrong to isolate most baby and young Christians in an artificial environment such as that of a "Christian Boarding Home" or a "Christian sanctuary" separated and isolated from life's regular mingles with the world. Unless a young Christian is trying to get away from some type of destructive addiction, then young Christians are to still be exposed to the world because though we are not of the world, we are in the world (John 17:14-16). Well-meaning and undiscerning Christians have taken young Christians under their wings, pampered them with a paternal attitude, and spoiled them for Christ and his church inside of some type of mission-compound or "Christian sanctuary" with no exposure to the world. Though this is a sincere approach, this is a sincerely wrong approach in trying to help young Christians grow!

In Deuteronomy 6:6-8, God gave us the instructions and format of where to disciple people. God said, *"And these words, which I command thee this day, shall be in thine heart: And thou shalt teach them diligently unto thy children, and shalt talk of them when thou sittest in thine house, and when thou walkest by the way, and when thou liest down, and when thou risest up. And thou shalt bind them for a sign upon thine hand, and they shall be as frontlets between thine eyes.*" God then repeated these same words five chapters later in Deuteronomy 11:18-20: "*Therefore shall ye lay up these my words in your heart and in your soul, and bind them for a sign upon your hand, that they may be as frontlets between your eyes. And ye shall teach them your children, speaking of them when thou sittest in thine house, and when thou walkest by the way, when thou liest down, and when thou risest up. And thou shalt write them upon the door posts of thine house, and upon thy gates:*" Why did God repeat this for us? I think for the purpose to show us that the place of discipleship or mentorship is not a mission compound, but it is within the local church and godly activities in the world that we live in. It is in fellowship that young Christians are discipled, not in isolation. It is in fellowship before the world that young Christians are discipled and trained to walk righteously before the wicked of the world. God said that we are to teach His Word to new Christians in our conversations with them while we sit, walk, lie down, and rise up. True discipleship occurs at anyplace (at home and along the way) and during anytime (from rising to lying down). The reason for biblical conversations in all of these normal daily activities and times is so that the Word of God can be engrafted in their own hearts. This format of discipleship is what takes God's Word and moves it from the head and down eighteen inches into the heart of an individual. Being in godly conversations with someone anytime and anyplace is what builds a godly relationship.

In every church there must be disciple makers, men with men and women with women. The pastor alone cannot disciple nor mentor young Christians. There must be trained men and women who can take the responsibility for the small Bible study groups and the personal involvement in other's lives. The entire congregation must be trained to share responsibility and to give Christian fellowship so that men and women can rise up and effectively do the works of ministry (Ephesians 4:12). Even young Christians who have had some training and experience in their Christian life and faith can be put to work in this way. They can be mentored to learn the responsibility of getting involved in another's life who needs to be loved on and brought closer to Jesus. Even recent converts can learn to begin to mentor brand-new Christians. In mentoring others, they themselves will learn to take their problems to the Lord for guidance for their questions and answers. In this way, they will also grow.

I mentioned a principle before, and I'll repeat it again. It is important to understand. A ratio of one pastor for 50, 100, or more people in a congregation is difficult and impossible to train people up in becoming effective disciple makers. The size of the congregation is irrelevant. Instead, you merely have to be selective as God portrayed in the Bible and as Jesus did in His ministry. For example, way back in time in the Old Testament, God exemplified discipleship through the children of Israel. When God originally planned how big the "Christian classroom" should be He assigned one tribe, the Levites, to minister to twelve tribes. Thus God originated the one to twelve (1/12) ratio. Years later when Jesus was on this planet and when He picked His ratio of men, He selected twelve men (Mark 3:14). Though one ended up being bad fruit, a man of perdition, Jesus chose the same one to twelve (1/12) ratio. Today, overseers of local congregations must implement the same God-inspired discipleship principle if they are going to effectively not only teach, but also train their flocks to be effective, efficient disciple makers. Overseers must select a few good men and women. For example, the pastor should organize a small group, even give the group a neat little name, if he so desires. He should meet up with them off the church property and at some other location, such as at his house or someone else's home. The small group should comprise of a few handpicked lay people who have demonstrated themselves to the ministry and care of others. The pastor can lead this small group in teaching and training of how to teach from the Word and how to disciple and/or mentor others more effectively. The pastor should have the mindset within himself that he is going to be dedicated to this small group for years until they come to the point that they are successfully discipling others around themselves. Their usual program with the pastor should be to study the Word, prayer, and sharing of experiences, problems, and encouragements of discipleship. To this effect, the people will learn from each other and become better disciple makers and mentors. To this select group the pastor should try to impart the very best of his knowledge and experiences, and train them in turn to go out to disciple others as he is doing. As a result, the pastor is discipling this few handpicked individuals, who in turn will go around to mentor and sometimes disciple another group of others and indeed these will learn to turn around and mentor and disciple others around them, and so forth. Many members of the congregation will end up being obedient men and women of God who are not just witnessing but who are also living out lives in the investment of other lives around them. The whole of the church will eventually become healthier and more efficient in ministering to people.

Perhaps a pastor who would like to implement such an idea shuns away from it because he is concerned with being criticized for seemingly showing favoritism to anyone in the church. There is good news. There is a way in which a pastor can start a little discipleship group without battling the problem of favoritism. I suggest that a pastor who has this concern should announce to his entire congregation on a Sunday morning that he is going to start and conduct a discipleship class at six o'clock each Monday morning for anyone who wants to come. Those who the pastor may have in mind would be excellent candidates to disciple, two or three men; he may want to privately approach them and encourage to attend. In addition, he did extend an invitation to the entire congregation, so he may be blessed to see one or two faithful persons who will start attending the discipleship "class" that he had not had in mind. Those who do not come cannot ever accuse the pastor of favoritism because everyone knew that a discipleship class was starting and everyone had the opportunity to come.

Naturally, only those who are spiritually hungry will show up. Later, two or three might drop out, but those who stay become the real leaders in a local church.

No matter what, personal attention to each individual is vitally important. Jesus worked with His disciples in public and group settings. He took them to the synagogues, to celebrations, to people's homes, and to other events. However, He also distinctively worked one-on-one with them. No two people are alike in this world, and no two disciples are alike. A disciple maker must understand that he needs to work with people in public and group settings, but he also needs to work with people on an individual basis. We use the same Bible passages and principles for all people, but we must distinctively teach them to individuals at times in different manners. For example, with some individuals you might be able to speak very directly with them and have a strong tone of voice in rebuke. With another individual, he might not be able to take a strong rebuke, so you might want to work with him in a gentler manner. Some individuals need to be built up and encouraged for a season, and others might need to be reproved and rebuked often for a season. You cannot apply the same method of teaching to each individual the same way. You have to be sensitive and understand each individual's personality, qualities, and characteristics. Again, no two people are alike in this world, and no two disciples are alike. If you do this, you will hurt people or you will not serve them to a full capacity and just be wasting their time and your time.

Jesus understood this and this is why he worked differently with each disciple. He was very direct and brassy with Peter most of the time but with John He demonstrated a more affectionate warming discipline.

If Jesus would have been very direct and brassy with John, John's mentality and personality would have been destroyed. If He would have been warm and soft towards Peter all the time, Peter would have remained out of control and become seriously worse in his demeanor and zealous character. Therefore, there is a need to have discernment and make discipleship very personal on an individual basis many times.

We see a passage of scripture where Peter was wondering why Jesus was handling John differently. Jesus had a very direct but important response to him that we can learn from. In John 21:20-22, the scripture says, *"Then Peter, turning about, seeth the disciple whom Jesus loved following; which also leaned on his breast at supper, and said, Lord, which is he that betrayeth thee? Peter seeing him saith to Jesus, Lord, and what shall this man do? Jesus saith unto him, If I will that he tarry till I come, what is that to thee? follow thou me."* In the verses before this passage of scripture, Jesus just finished having a good private conversation with Peter on the beach. Jesus just finished encouraging Peter and assuring him that He wanted Peter to continue His mission and go feed His sheep. No later than right after this good time together, Peter turns around (vs. 20) and asks Jesus what He was going to do with John (vs. 21). More or less, Peter was putting his nose into something that was none of his business. Though it might seem that it was just a simple question of curiosity, Jesus responded to him, probably in a softer tone of rebuke, *"[W]hat is that to thee? follow thou me."* In other words, Jesus was conveying to him, that it was none of his business. Or, that it was nothing for him to worry about. Don't worry. Stop putting your nose in other people's business. I'll work with John the way I know is best and how I see fit. I work with you one way, and I work with him another way. Just be concerned with what I say to you and how I handle you.

As you see, Jesus worked with all of His disciples in group settings and in group interactions amongst people with Him. However, at other times, Jesus met alone with His disciples and distinctively worked with them in private matters.

We should work with people in group settings and in one-on-one settings too so that we can help them become all that God would have them to become. A loving parent works with children publicly and privately. We should have a heart and actions of a loving parent.

Even the Apostle Paul had this kind of heart for those he worked with. To the Thessalonians believers, he wrote in 1 Thessalonians 2:11: *"As ye know how we exhorted and comforted and charged every one of you, as a father doth his children."* Like a father, we need to work with people not only in their spiritual life, but amongst their physical and emotional life too. Sometimes we might want to meet with an individual alone and help him learn about common sense mistakes like debt, cleanliness, dress, bad relationships, and other normal things of life. We need to be meek, gracious, and have an attitude of lowliness while we talk with them. We do all of this so that they can be built up and become a stronger individual in the world who is dependent on God, has strong ethics, and common sense. Care must always be taken that the new believers do not depend completely on the one who disciples them. God's order of things is that all will come to become dependent on Him alone. When a man becomes a necessity to another individual, he has moved out of God's order. Therefore, we are to guide young Christians to know Jesus and only to become dependent on Him, not on us, because there may come a time in our lives in which the disciple maker and the disciple may become separated, because of either death or geographical relocation, and not see each other again.

We have gobs of Christians who have been used to just being fed and they do not know how to go to God, spend time with Him in the Word, and be fed everyday from Him. This should not be. All of this reminds me of an old saying that goes, "Give someone a fish and feed him for a day or TEACH a person to fish and feed him for a lifetime." We need to take the thrust we have on teaching knowledge and direct it toward teaching people, such as young Christians, to feed themselves (Ezra 7:10) directly from God. Teaching knowledge should not be stopped, but self-feeding should receive a greater focus. We do not want to fish for a man in order to feed him, but we want to teach him how to fish (how to spend quality time with God) so that he can feed himself; for a time will arise in the future when we are long gone.

I hope that you see what a high calling we have! We are not only commissioned to preach the Gospel message of our Lord Jesus Christ to the world, but after someone decides to begin a new relationship with God, we are to then disciple and mentor these new converts. We are to disciple and mentor men and women to love and serve our Lord Jesus Christ and His church! Jesus has authorized us and ordered us in Matthew 28:19-20 to go out and get involved in other people's lives, to go and make disciples. God's Word lets us know in 1 Corinthians 14:12 that those of us who are eager for gifts which manifest the power of God's Spirit should seek to excel in building up the church. This is what discipleship is all about. Not only is the work of discipleship obedience to the Word, but it is God's plan to make the work of teaching and training more simple, more effective, and more efficient in the long run of built up believers.

So please, make the time to get involved in another's life. One must pay a price to be an effective, proficient disciple maker. The responsibility is yours!

PART FOUR

FURTHER EXHORTATIONS

CHAPTER 14
So Run the Race

For it is God which worketh in you both to will and to do of his good pleasure. Do all things without murmurings and disputings: That ye may be blameless and harmless, the sons of God, without rebuke, in the midst of a crooked and perverse nation, among whom ye shine as lights in the world; Holding forth the word of life; that I may rejoice in the day of Christ, that I have not run in vain, neither laboured in vain.
– Philippians 2:13-16

After reading this book, along with the other books of this soulwinning series, there is a big possibility that there may be some of you who may wish that I had gone into greater detail on some matters and less on others. I understand this is a reality and for that, my explanation is that it is difficult to envision every possible situation, as you would imagine. What I have tried to do within the scope of these books is to include truth, material, and information that can be used as a foundation or as a basis for you to learn from and implement into your life so that you can build upon these words and do greater works with the Lord.

There is a big possibility that some of the material that I have placed in these books may not be relevant to your situation at the present moment. For this, I say, "Don't worry." A time may arise in which some material that you find you cannot use right now, may come in handy in the future. Just be patient and do not forget what you have learned. Store those truths in the back of your heart through meditation on God's Word. Moreover, be ready to use them when the appropriate situation arises.

Still, there is possibly some material that is not suited for your particular work, service, or ministry. You have read the material and though something was valuable and attractive as an idea, for whatever reason you think it cannot be adopted in your case. If that is the case, do not be discouraged. Though there may be some things in this book that you think you cannot adopt, you may eventually find ways to adapt some of them in your life and ministry. For the time being, be challenged, exhorted, and encouraged to still rise up and implement what you know to do.

Most certainly, I will not have the opportunity to meet most of the people who read my books. However, I pray that the words of this book will stimulate you to take action in three means. First, I prayerfully hope that you will seek the Lord Jesus on a daily basis through being in His Word and in fervent prayer so that you will increase in knowing Him. Second, I hope that you will demonstrate your appreciation of what He has done for you through daily choosing actions that please Him. Lastly, I hope that you will continue to study and learn how to more effectively soulwin. Keep in mind the Apostle Paul's exhortation in 1 Corinthians 9:24 and Hebrews 12:1b, "*Know ye not that they which run in a race run all, but one receiveth the prize? So run, that ye may obtain. [A]nd let us run with patience the race that is set before us.*" Remember, you are in a race. Your greatest opponent is yourself. So, run, be persistent, and run with obedience through patience; and run through experiencing God daily in His Word, prayer, and in the lives of people.

Let this book, along with the other books in this series serve as a reference to methods that have worked around the world and are based on the teachings of the Holy Bible, God's Word. May the Holy Spirit use it to rise up thousands of spiritually qualified workers for the glory of Jesus Christ.

Amen!

CHAPTER 15
Suggested Books to Read

Study to shew thyself approved unto God, a workman that needeth not
to be ashamed, rightly dividing the word of truth.
– 2 Timothy 2:15

In leaving you with this book and its contents, I also desire to give you some suggestions of other literature that you might like to pick up to read. Proverbs 23:23 instructs us to, *"Buy the truth, and sell it not; also wisdom, and instruction, and understanding."* In so following this instruction, I strongly suggest some books for you to buy that could be a help to you as they have been a help to me. The following books can be used to teach and equip you with additional knowledge and wisdom from the Word of God concerning the particulars of soulwinning. While I do not personally know any of these writers at the time of this writing, their writings have been a tremendous valuable resource in my life, along with God's Word. I recommend you to go buy them, so you can have them in your personal library for reference. Do read them along with your Holy Bible right next to the book. That way you can readily look up and meditate on any scripture that they mention inside their books. Most importantly, apply any principles into your life that God reveals to you. The more you study and apply His Word in your life, the more you will come to know God and you will be richly blessed. God will richly bless you in more intimacy with Him and give you fruit to encourage you and allow you to experience Him being glorified.

After you leave this world and pass on into Heaven, if you shall find as one of your rewards beloved individuals to welcome you into glory land; it will add additional incomprehensible ecstasies of joys to your own eternal joys, to meet people who shall salute you as their teacher

205

who brought them to Jesus. In light of this anticipation, I would not wish to go to Heaven alone—would you? I would not wish to stand before Jesus at His throne and not have people to show before Him how much I appreciated His sacrificial outpouring of His blood—would you? Therefore, take the power of His bloodshed from the stripes on His body, the marks on His hands and feet, and *"go ye into all the world, and preach the Gospel to every creature;"* and be encouraged to know this that James 5:20 says, *"he which converteth the sinner from the error of his way shall save a soul from death, and shall hide a multitude of sins."*

Now, may you enjoy your future endeavors with God in personal studies and personal involvement in the lives of people.

Suggested Books to Read

Born to Reproduce
By: Dawson E. Trotman

The Lost Art of Disciple Making
By: LeRoy Eims

As Iron Sharpens Iron
By: Howard Hendricks and William Hendricks

Leaders Guide for Evangelistic Bible Studies
(Using the Gospel of John)
By: The Navigators®

How To Witness To Anyone
By: Reuben A. Torrey

Any literature or books written by:
LeRoy Eims, Charles Finney, John R. Rice,
Charles H. Spurgeon, or Dawson E. Trotman

Notes

For they have refreshed my spirit and yours: therefore
acknowledge ye them that are such.
−1 Corinthians 16:18

I have compiled this *Notes* section of my book for you the reader. In case you desire more readings of a specific topic after you read a chapter, you can view below to see which books, websites, literatures, or people I used to assist me in writing the particular chapter. Though I have used different authors for various references, I respectfully would like to inform you that I may or may not necessarily agree with all of their biblical viewpoints, opinions, beliefs, and teachings.

CHAPTER 1 : My Story

Curington, Steven B. *Reformers Unanimous 10 Principles Videos*. San Diego, California, USA: Winter 2010. DVD Video.

CHAPTER 2 : What Is Soulwinning?

Adsit, Christopher B. *Personal Disciplemaking: A Step-by-step Guide for Leading a Christian From New Birth to Maturity*. Orlando, Florida, USA: Campus Crusade for Christ. 1996. Print. Page 28

"Go." *Webster's Encyclopedic Unabridged Dictionary of the English Language*. New York, New York USA: Gramercy Books 1996. Print. Page 816.

Hopewell Baptist Church, and Mike Ray. "Step 7 SOULWINNING." *One Step At A Time*. Pasig City, M.M. Philippians: Life Line Philippians Baptist Foundation. Print. Page 1.

Hyles, Jack. *Let's Build An Evangelistic Church*. Murfreesboro, Tennessee, USA.: Sword of the Lord Publishers, 1962. Print. Pages 31-32

Jordan, Doug. The Lighthouse Baptist Church, San Diego, California, USA: Spring 2010. Preaching.

Mount Zion Bible Church. "Unabridged and Unedited, Delivered in the Year 1869, at the METROPOLITAN TABERNACLE, NEWINGTON, Soulwinning CH Spurgeon." *Chapel Library: Mount Zion Baptist Church:*. Mount Zion Baptist Church. Web. Winter 2010. <http://www.biblebb.com/files/spurgeon/0850.htm>.

"Practical Preaching Principles." *Soulwinning*. Web. Winter 2009. < http://www. soulwinning.info/sp/lessons/04.htm >.

Schindler, Fred. "Get Committed! Go Soulwinning! - Dr. Fred Schindler." *The Sword of the Lord Publishers*. Web. Fall 2009. <http://www.swordofthelord.com/onlinesermons/CommittedSoulWinning.htm>.

Spurgeon, Charles H. *The Soul-winner: How to Lead Sinners to the Saviour*. Grand Rapids, Michigan, USA: Eerdmans Publishing, 1974. Print. Page 45.

Stewart, David J. *Soulwinning*. Web. Winter 2009. <http://www.soulwinning.info>.

"Teach." *Webster's Encyclopedic Unabridged Dictionary of the English Language*. New York, New York USA: Gramercy Books 1996. Print. Page 1948.

CHAPTER 3 : What Is the Gospel of Jesus Christ?

Adsit, Christopher B. *Personal Disciplemaking: A Step-by-step Guide for Leading a Christian From New Birth to Maturity*. Orlando, Florida, USA: Campus Crusade for Christ. 1996. Print. Page 129.

Bible Baptist Church. *The Gospel*. Oak Harbor, Washington: Bible Baptist Church Publications, 2001. Gospel Track. Print.

"Gospel." *Wikipedia, the Free Encyclopedia.* 18 Oct. 2010. Web. 23 Oct. 2010. <http://en.wikipedia.org/wiki/Gospel>.

Hughes, R. Kent. *Disciplines of a Godly Man.* Wheaton, Illinois, USA.: Crossway Books, 2006. Print. Pages 87, 227.

"Ransom." Webster, Noah, and Rosalie J. Slater. *Noah Webster's First Edition of an American Dictionary of the English Language 1828.* San Francisco, Calif.: Foundation for American Christian Education, 1995. Sixteenth Printing, 2004. C.J. Krehbiel Company, Cincinnati, Ohio USA. Print. Volume II, Page 50.

"Redeem." Webster, Noah, and Rosalie J. Slater. *Noah Webster's First Edition of an American Dictionary of the English Language 1828.* San Francisco, Calif.: Foundation for American Christian Education, 1995. Sixteenth Printing, 2004. C.J. Krehbiel Company, Cincinnati, Ohio USA. Print. Volume II, Page 52.

Welch, Charles H. "RIGHT DIVISION." Http://www.charleswelch.net/books.htm. Web. 21 Feb. 2011. <http://www.bibleunderstanding.com/RIGHT%20DIVISION.PDF>.

CHAPTER 4 : Two Ways You Witness

Hopewell Baptist Church, and Mike Ray. "Step 7 SOULWINNING." *One Step At A Time.* Pasig City, M.M. Philippians: Life Line Philippians Baptist Foundation. Print. Page 3.

Hughes, R. Kent. *Disciplines of a Godly Man.* Wheaton, Illinois, USA.: Crossway Books, 2006. Print. Page 139.

"Preach." *Webster's Encyclopedic Unabridged Dictionary of the English Language.* New York, New York USA: Gramercy Books 1996. Print. Page 1519.

CHAPTER 5 : Baptism

"Baptism." Berry, George Ricker, and George Ricker Berry. *Berry's Interlinear Greek-English New Testament: with a Greek- English Lexicon and New Testament Synonyms.* Grand Rapids, Michigan, USA.: Baker Book House, 1897. Print.

"Baptism." Thayer, Joseph Henry, Carl Ludwig Wilibald Grimm, and Christian Gottlob Wilke. *Thayer's Greek-English Lexicon of the New Testament: Coded with the Numbering System from Strong's Exhaustive Concordance of the Bible.* Peabody, Massachusetts, USA.: Hendrickson, 1981. Print. Page 94.

"Baptize." Berry, George Ricker, and George Ricker Berry. *Berry's Interlinear Greek-English New Testament: with a Greek- English Lexicon and New Testament Synonyms.* Grand Rapids, Michigan, USA.: Baker Book House, 1897. Print.

"Baptize." Strong, James, and James Strong. *The New Strong's Exhaustive Concordance of the Bible: with Main Concordance, Appendix to the Main Concordance, Key Verse Comparison Chart, Dictionary of the Hebrew Bible, Dictionary of the Greek Testament.* Nashville, Tennessee, USA.: Thomas Nelson, 1984. Print.

"Baptize." Thayer, Joseph Henry, Carl Ludwig Wilibald Grimm, and Christian Gottlob Wilke. *Thayer's Greek-English Lexicon of the New Testament: Coded with the Numbering System from Strong's Exhaustive Concordance of the Bible.* Peabody, Massachusetts, USA.: Hendrickson, 1981. Print. Page 95.

Ryrie, Charles C. *Ryrie Study Bible Expanded Edition: King James Version.* Chicago, Illinois, USA: Moody Press, 1994. Print. Page 1478.

"What Is Baptism?" *Clarifying Christianity.* Clarifying Christianity (SM). Web. 17 May 2010. <http://www.clarifyingchristianity.com/get_wet.shtml>.

"Whelm." Webster, Noah, and Rosalie J. Slater. *Noah Webster's First Edition of an American Dictionary of the English Language 1828.* San Francisco, Calif.: Foundation for American Christian Education, 1995. Sixteenth Printing, 2004. C.J. Krehbiel Company, Cincinnati, Ohio USA. Print. Volume II, Page 112.

NOTES

CHAPTER 6 : A Soulwinner Is to Follow-up with Young Christians

Perry, David. The University of Rio Grande, Rio Grande, Ohio, USA: Fall 1998-Spring 2003. Lecture.

Perry, David. Various messages to the author. 2005-2010. E-mail

Williams, Theodore. "Nuturing And Discipling New Converts." *Let the Earth Hear His Voice: the Complete Papers from the International Congress on World Evangelization, Lausanne, 1974.* By J. D. Douglas. London, England: World Wide Publishers. 1974. Print. Pages 574-579.

CHAPTER 7 : The Basis of Investing Your Life into Others

Adsit, Christopher B. *Personal Disciplemaking: A Step-by-step Guide for Leading a Christian From New Birth to Maturity.* Orlando, Florida, USA: Campus Crusade for Christ. 1996. Print. Page 51, 57.

Eims, LeRoy. *The Lost Art of Disciple Making.* Grand Rapids, Michigan, USA: Zondervan, 1984. Print. Page 136.

Lancaster, Philip. *Family Man, Family Leader.* San Antonio, Texas, USA: The Vision Forum, Inc., 2004. Print. Pages 43, 291.

Perry, David. The University of Rio Grande, Rio Grande, Ohio, USA: Fall 1998-Spring 2003. Lecture.

Perry, David. Various messages to the author. 2005-2010. E-mail

Williams, Theodore. "Nuturing And Discipling New Converts." *Let the Earth Hear His Voice: the Complete Papers from the International Congress on World Evangelization, Lausanne, 1974.* By J. D. Douglas. London, England: World Wide Publishers. Print. Pages 574-579.

CHAPTER 8 : There Is a Great Need

Hughes, R. Kent. *Disciplines of a Godly Man*. Wheaton, Illinois, USA.: Crossway Books, 2006. Print. Page 218.

Northcutt, Scott. The Lighthouse Baptist Church, San Diego, California, USA: Winter 2010. Preaching.

Perry, David. The University of Rio Grande, Rio Grande, Ohio, USA: Fall 1998-Spring 2003. Lecture.

Perry, David. Various messages to the author. 2005-2010. E-mail

Williams, Theodore. "Nuturing And Discipling New Converts." *Let the Earth Hear His Voice: the Complete Papers from the International Congress on World Evangelization, Lausanne, 1974.* By J. D. Douglas. London, England: World Wide Publishers. 1974. Print. Pages 574-579.

CHAPTER 9 : The Differences Between Discipling and Mentoring

Adsit, Christopher B. *Personal Disciplemaking: A Step-by-step Guide for Leading a Christian From New Birth to Maturity*. Orlando, Florida, USA: Campus Crusade for Christ. 1996. Print. Page 38,83-84.

Eims, LeRoy. *The Lost Art of Disciple Making*. Grand Rapids, Michigan, USA: Zondervan, 1984. Print. Page 105.

Perry, David. The University of Rio Grande, Rio Grande, Ohio, USA: Fall 1998-Spring 2003. Lecture.

Perry, David. Various messages to the author. 2005-2010. E-mail

Williams, Theodore. "Nuturing And Discipling New Converts." *Let the Earth Hear His Voice: the Complete Papers from the International Congress on World Evangelization,*

Lausanne, 1974. By J. D. Douglas. London, England: World Wide Publishers. 1974. Print. Pages 574-579.

CHAPTER 10 : The Objectives of Discipling and Mentoring

"Beguile." Webster, Noah, and Rosalie J. Slater. *Noah Webster's First Edition of an American Dictionary of the English Language 1828.* San Francisco, Calif.: Foundation for American Christian Education, 1995. Sixteenth Printing, 2004. C.J. Krehbiel Company, Cincinnati, Ohio USA. Print. Volume I, Page 20.

Perry, David. The University of Rio Grande, Rio Grande, Ohio, USA: Fall 1998-Spring 2003. Lecture.

Perry, David. Various messages to the author. 2005-2010. E-mail

Williams, Theodore. "Nuturing And Discipling New Converts." *Let the Earth Hear His Voice: the Complete Papers from the International Congress on World Evangelization, Lausanne, 1974.* By J. D. Douglas. London, England: World Wide Publishers. Print. Pages 574-579.

CHAPTER 11 : Start Investing Your Life into Someone Today

Adsit, Christopher B. *Personal Disciplemaking: A Step-by-step Guide for Leading a Christian From New Birth to Maturity.* Orlando, Florida, USA: Campus Crusade for Christ. 1996. Print. Page 85-86, 99, 109-110.

Bean, Cecil. Letter to David Perry. 1995. MS. Rio Grande, Ohio, USA.

Eims, LeRoy. *The Lost Art of Disciple Making.* Grand Rapids, Michigan, USA: Zondervan, 1984. Print. Pages 102, 136, 155.

Perry, David. The University of Rio Grande, Rio Grande, Ohio, USA: Fall 1998-Spring 2003. Lecture.

Perry, David. Various messages to the author. 2005-2010. E-mail

Williams, Theodore. "Nuturing And Discipling New Converts." *Let the Earth Hear His Voice: the Complete Papers from the International Congress on World Evangelization, Lausanne, 1974.* By J. D. Douglas. London, England: World Wide Publishers. Print. Pages 574-579.

CHAPTER 12 : Teach and Train the Basics of what a Young Christian Needs to Know

Perry, David. The University of Rio Grande, Rio Grande, Ohio, USA: Fall 1998-Spring 2003. Lecture.

Perry, David. Various messages to the author. 2005-2010. E-mail

Williams, Theodore. "Nuturing And Discipling New Converts." *Let the Earth Hear His Voice: the Complete Papers from the International Congress on World Evangelization, Lausanne, 1974.* By J. D. Douglas. London, England: World Wide Publishers. 1974. Print. Pages 574-579.

CHAPTER 13 : The Responsibility Is Yours

Eims, LeRoy. *The Lost Art of Disciple Making.* Grand Rapids, Michigan, USA: Zondervan, 1984. Print. Pages 155-156.

Lancaster, Philip. *Family Man, Family Leader.* San Antonio, Texas, USA: The Vision Forum, Inc., 2004. Print.Pages 140-141,144-145, 195-198.

Perry, David. The University of Rio Grande, Rio Grande, Ohio, USA: Fall 1998-Spring 2003. Lecture.

Perry, David. Various messages to the author. 2005-2010. E-mail

Williams, Theodore. "Nuturing And Discipling New Converts." *Let the Earth Hear His Voice: the Complete Papers from the International Congress on World Evangelization, Lausanne, 1974.* By J. D. Douglas. London, England: World Wide Publishers. 1974. Print. Pages 574-579.

CHAPTER 14 : So Run The Race

Eims, LeRoy. *The Lost Art of Disciple Making*. Grand Rapids, Michigan, USA: Zondervan, 1984. Print. Page 157.

Spurgeon, Charles H. *The Soul-winner: How to Lead Sinners to the Saviour*. Grand Rapids, Michigan, USA: Eerdmans Publishing, 1974. Print. Pages 318-319.

Bibliography

For they have refreshed my spirit and yours: therefore
acknowledge ye them that are such.
– 1 Corinthians 16:18

Adsit, Christopher B. *Personal Disciplemaking: A Step-by-step Guide for Leading a Christian From New Birth to Maturity.* Orlando, Florida, USA: Campus Crusade for Christ. 1996. Print.

Bean, Cecil. Letter to David Perry. 1995. MS. Rio Grande, Ohio, USA.

Berry, George Ricker, and George Ricker Berry. *Berry's Interlinear Greek-English New Testament: with a Greek- English Lexicon and New Testament Synonyms.* Grand Rapids, Michigan, USA.: Baker Book House, 1897. Print.

Bible Baptist Church. *The Gospel.* Oak Harbor, Washington: Bible Baptist Church Publications, 2001. Gospel Track. Print.

Curington, Steven B. *Reformers Unanimous 10 Principles Videos.* San Diego, California, USA: Winter 2010. DVD Video.

Eims, LeRoy. *The Lost Art of Disciple Making.* Grand Rapids, Michigan, USA: Zondervan, 1984. Print

"Gospel." *Wikipedia, the Free Encyclopedia.* 18 Oct. 2010. Web. 23 Oct. 2010. <http://en.wikipedia.org/wiki/Gospel>.

Hopewell Baptist Church, and Mike Ray. "Step 7 SOULWINNING." *One Step At A Time.* Pasig City, M.M. Philippians: Life Line Philippians Baptist Foundation. Print.

Hughes, R. Kent. *Disciplines of a Godly Man*. Wheaton, Illinois, USA.: Crossway Books, 2006. Print.

Hyles, Jack. *Let's Build An Evangelistic Church*. Murfreesboro, Tennessee, USA.: Sword of the Lord Publishers, 1962. Print.

Jordan, Doug. The Lighthouse Baptist Church, San Diego, California, USA: Spring 2010. Preaching.

Lancaster, Philip. *Family Man, Family Leader*. San Antonio, Texas, USA: The Vision Forum, Inc., 2004. Print.

Mount Zion Bible Church. "Unabridged and Unedited, Delivered in the Year 1869, at the METROPOLITAN TABERNACLE, NEWINGTON, Soulwinning CH Spurgeon." *Chapel Library: Mount Zion Baptist Church:*. Mount Zion Baptist Church. Web. Winter 2010.

Northcutt, Scott. The Lighthouse Baptist Church, San Diego, California, USA: Winter 2010. Preaching.

Perry, David. The University of Rio Grande, Rio Grande, Ohio, USA: Fall 1998-Spring 2003. Lecture.

Perry, David. Various messages to the author. 2005-2010. E-mail

"Practical Preaching Principles." *Soulwinning*. Web. Winter 2009. < http://www.soulwinning.info/sp/lessons/04.htm >.

Ryrie, Charles C. *Ryrie Study Bible Expanded Edition: King James Version*. Chicago, Illinois, USA: Moody Press, 1994. Print.

Schindler, Fred. "Get Committed! Go Soulwinning! - Dr. Fred Schindler." *The Sword of the Lord Publishers*. Web. Fall 2009. <http://www.swordofthelord.com/onlinesermons/CommittedSoulWinning.htm>.

BIBLIOGRAPHY

Spurgeon, Charles H. *The Soul-winner: How to Lead Sinners to the Saviour*. Grand Rapids, Michigan, USA: Eerdmans Publishing, 1974. Print.

Stewart, David J. "How to Win a Soul to Christ." *Soulwinning*. Web. Winter 2009. <http://www.soulwinning.info/articles/how_to.htm>.

Strong, James, and James Strong. *The New Strong's Exhaustive Concordance of the Bible: with Main Concordance, Appendix to the Main Concordance, Key Verse Comparison Chart, Dictionary of the Hebrew Bible, Dictionary of the Greek Testament*. Nashville, Tennessee, USA.: Thomas Nelson, 1984. Print.

Thayer, Joseph Henry, Carl Ludwig Wilibald Grimm, and Christian Gottlob Wilke. *Thayer's Greek-English Lexicon of the New Testament: Coded with the Numbering System from Strong's Exhaustive Concordance of the Bible*. Peabody, Massachusetts, USA.: Hendrickson, 1981. Print.

Webster's Encyclopedic Unabridged Dictionary of the English Language. New York, New York USA: Gramercy Books 1996. Print.

Webster, Noah, and Rosalie J. Slater. *Noah Webster's First Edition of an American Dictionary of the English Language 1828*. San Francisco, Calif.: Foundation for American Christian Education, 1995. Sixteenth Printing, 2004. C.J. Krehbiel Company, Cincinnati, Ohio USA. Print.

Welch, Charles H. "RIGHT DIVISION." Http://www.charleswelch.net/books.htm. Web. 21 Feb. 2011. <http://www.bibleunderstanding.com/RIGHT%20DIVISION.PDF>.

"What Is Baptism?" *Clarifying Christianity*. Clarifying Christianity (SM). Web. 17 May 2010. <http://www.clarifyingchristianity.com/get_wet.shtml>.

Williams, Theodore. "Nuturing And Discipling New Converts." *Let the Earth Hear His Voice: the Complete Papers from the International Congress on World Evangelization, Lausanne, 1974*. By J. D. Douglas. London, England: World Wide Pubs, 1974. 574-79. Print.

Mr. Bowman would love to hear from you. If you have any questions, concerns, if you notice any mistakes inside this book, or if you desire to inquire about other resources by Lawrence Bowman, you are invited to contact him at:

www.GoSoulwinning.com

or

www.LawrenceBowman.com

Thank you.

Made in the USA
Monee, IL
21 April 2021